Investment and Speculation
with
WARRANTS·OPTIONS
&
CONVERTIBLES
by Sidney Fried

Investment and Speculation
with
WARRANTS·OPTIONS
&
CONVERTIBLES
by Sidney Fried

Library of Congress No. 89-38021

ISBN 0-89058-606-3

R.H.M. Press
172 Forest Avenue
Glen Cove, New York 11542

To my beloved son

Grant Ellis Fried

INDEX OPTIONS

How a 1987 investment in the February 255 Call Index Options saw **$1,062** become worth **$69,000** in seven weeks.

It is January 1987, and as Editor of a well-known investment service covering the Options and Warrants field, we are expecting a rising market. Consequently, we recommend purchase of the "February 255 Call Options" for the "S & P 100 Index," using "Dollar Averaging."

(Note: **Call** Index Options profit when the stock market moves *higher*. **Dollar Averaging** is the purchase of approximately equal dollar amounts of Index Options as they move lower in price.)

Our experience has been that Dollar Averaging begins best around the 1/2 (50 cents) level, at which time a typical purchase is, say, $500 for 10 Options at 1/2. Having made this purchase, open orders are given to one's broker to buy *equal dollar amounts* on a scale down, as follows:

$500 for *20* Options at 1/4

$500 for *40* Options at 1/8

$500 for *80* Options at 1/16

In this case, the process began by purchasing 10

February 255 Call Options at *9/16* for $562. (Whether we begin at 9/16 or 5/8, or at 1/2, the next scheduled purchase is always at 1/4, then at 1/8, and then at 1/16, if the Option gets that low.)

The February 255 Call Options did indeed reach 1/4 as the market first declined, whereupon 20 Options were purchased for $500, but at this point the market began to move higher, so no further purchases were made.

We had purchased 10 Options at 9/16 for $562;

We had purchased 20 Options at 1/4 for $500;

We now owned 30 February 255 Call Options, which had cost a total of *$1,062.*

When the first 10 February 255 Call Options were purchased at 9/16, the Standard & Poor's 100 Index, on which the Option was based, stood at *235.90.*

This meant that the Index (as a measure of the stock market as a whole) would have to rise *19.10 points* before the Option would begin to develop value. *Beyond* 255 — which is the "Strike" Price — each point of further advance in the S & P 100 Index would add $100 in value per Option.

So if you owned *30* February 255 Call Options, each point advance in the Index beyond 255 would add *$3,000* in value.

The S & P 100 Index is an "average" of 100 leading

stocks, just as the famed Dow Jones Industrial Average is an "average" of 30 leading stocks. Therefore, when you buy a Call Option, you are speculating that the general market will move *up*.

An Index Option has a maximum life of three months. If the market does not advance sufficiently after you have made your purchase, you lose the entire investment. But if the market *does* start an upside run of some dimensions, the profit can be spectacular, and is *always* large.

And that is just what happened with the S & P 100 Index, which reached as high as *278* in the last week of life for the Option. At 278, the 255 Call Option is worth *23*, and that is where the Option sold.

At 23, one Option is worth $2,300, and since our position held *30* Options, those Options were worth *$69,000*.

The investment in 30 February 255 Call Options had seen **$1,062** become worth **$69,000** in seven weeks.

The October 285 PUT Index Options

These few paragraphs are but an introduction to the whole subject of successful speculation with Index Options, and in later pages we will describe how we did correctly anticipate, in the pages of the **R.H.M. Survey**, the savage decline in the market during October 1987, and how we consequently recommended purchase of the October 285 *Put* Index Options. (Note: *Put* Index Options profit when the stock market moves *down*.)

13

In this instance, Dollar Averaging went the whole way from 5/8 to 1/16, and our position had *148* Put Options, which had cost *$2,000*.

On October 16, 1987, the Friday before the October 19th crash, the S & P 100 Index fell 15.95 points to *274.13*. Having sold as low as *273.52* on that day, the *285* Put Index Options were worth 285 minus 273.52, or 11.48, and actually sold as high as *13*.

With one Option being worth $1,300 at 13, *148* Options were worth *$192,400*.

A **$2,000** investment had become worth **$192,400** in six weeks, with the October 285 Put Index Options.

Note: On later pages we will be describing specifically how a profitable Index Option receives a cash payment for that profit, and exactly why and how an Index Option will move up, or down, with the movement of the general market. For the time being, we are presenting these first examples without that necessary understanding.

The Logical Basis of INTELLIGENT Index Option Speculation

The February 255 Call Index Options and the October 285 Put Index Options both showed very large profits, but there had been other substantial profits with both Call Options and Put Options in the pages of the **R.H.M. Survey** throughout recent years.

There also were *losses*, and the number of individual losses were *greater* than the number of gains. Did that negate the concept? Not at all! All the individual losses, by definition, had to be very *small*, while when a success was scored, the profits ranged from large to *very* large.

Thus, we favor using $500 units of purchase with Index Option speculation, though individuals may use smaller, or larger, units, depending on their financial circumstances.

(Here we are referring only to *initial* investments. In *Pyramiding*, larger sums come into play, when we are risking not original capital, but *profits*.)

With initial $500 units, the *maximum* investment, if Dollar Averaging gets down to 1/16 as the last purchase, is *$2,000*. And if only two purchases are made before a reversal, the total investment is only *$1,000*. Yet, when one success is scored, the profit can easily run to tens of thousands of dollars.

Maximum losses of $500 to $2,000 on individual commitments;

Profits-without-limit, typically amounting to tens of thousands of dollars.

It is obvious that if one has sufficient forbearance to *accept* two, three or four losses, and to utilize the all-important techniques of "Technical Analysis" (market timing analysis), the successes that often *do* obtain will easily wipe out all the preceding small losses and end up with a *large*, sometimes a *very* large net profit.

Pyramiding

A most important approach we recommend is called "Pyramiding," and is uniquely applicable to speculation with Index Options. In this approach, we utilize part of the profits of one success to increase the size of the next commitment in which case, *super* profits can develop.

Let us look at one example of a possible Pyramiding, which we do not necessarily recommend except for speculators that have "iron nerves" (!), but which will illustrate the *super leverage* of the concept.

In the last 10 days-or-so of the life of an Index Option, an Option which is not too far from its exercise (or "Strike") price often sells at a lowly 1/16. If there is a sudden movement in the market in those intervening 10 days — such as with "Futures-Related Program Trading," which we explain on later pages — speculative excitement can push that Option from 1/16 to 1 quite easily, even if the Option still has not reached its Strike Price.

When that happens, full or partial profits can be taken.

An investment in 100 Index Options at 1/16 costs *$625.* If the Index Option reaches 1, the 100 Options are worth *$10,000.*

You now wait for what appeals to you as being another well-timed opportunity to buy at 1/16, with the Option, again, not too far from its Strike Price, and the potential for a market "reversal," which is typically the key to a success.

Only this time you buy *1,000* Options at 1/16, which costs *$6,250*. You still have $3,750 left from your profit on the previous $625 to $10,000 success.

If another 1/16 to 1 success is achieved, the 1,000 Options at 1 are worth *$100,000*.

$625 has become *$100,000* through a two-step successful Pyramiding.

In this instance, if you suffer a loss on the commitment, you lose $625. But whenever the Pyramiding *succeeds*, there is a $100,000 profit.

Clearly, you can suffer a *long* string of losses, each representing a loss of $625, but *one* success, in bringing in $100,000, will hardly see that profit diminished much by a string of $625 losses. Even 10 such losses in a row only amounts to a total loss of $6,250.

One need not enter into such an all-out speculation in Pyramiding. For example, if one success has seen $625 becoming worth $10,000 as the Option went from 1/16 to 1, the next commitment could be, say, *50* Index Options at 1/16 for *$3,125*.

17

To close this introduction to Index Options with a recent "1/16 to 1" move, we had been analyzing the action (1989) of the May Call Index Options in the pages of the **R.H.M. Survey**, and two tables from our discussion (both courtesy of the **Wall Street Journal**) demonstrate the manner in which such a "1/16 to 1" move develops.

(Note, at this time, and throughout the book, that although it is very desirable to have a chart, or other graphic presentation on the same page, or a facing page,

---

Thursday, May 11, 1989

OPTIONS
Chicago Board

S&P 100 INDEX

Strike Price -	Calls—Last			Puts—Last		
	May	Jun	Jul	May	Jun	Jul
240	....	....	....	1/16	....	....
255	....	....	....	1/16	....	....
260	....	....	30⅞	1/16	7/16	15/16
265	....	....	....	⅛	⅝	1⅜
270	17¾	19¼	22¼	¼	1	2
275	12¾	15	....	7/16	1⅝	2¾
280	8	11	13¾	⅞	2⅝	3⅞
285	4	7½	10¾	2 1/16	4¼	5¾
290	1½	4⅝	7¾	4⅝	6⅝	7⅝
295	7/16	2⅝	5¼	8¾	9⅝	10½
300 ──►	1/16	1⅜	3⅜	13¾	14¼	14⅛
305	....	⅝	2⅛	....	19	....

Total call volume 57,239   Total call open int. 341,098
Total put volume 75,097   Total put open int. 426,514
The index: High 287.08; Low 285.76; Close 286.67, +0.86.

it is not always possible to have that outcome. So, if there are times when you must turn a page to study a chart or other graphic, and then turn back to the discussion of same, please be aware that this inconvenience was unavoidable,)

Note for the May 11, 1989 close, that with the S & P 100 Index at 286.67, the May 300 Call (arrow) was selling at 1/16. At the time, the Option was about 13 points "out of the money," or, to put it another way, the Strike Price (300) was 13 points higher than the Index Price (287).

Friday, May 19, 1989

OPTIONS

Chicago Board

S&P 100 INDEX

Strike Price	Calls—Last			Puts—Last		
	May	Jun	Jul	May	Jun	Jul
260	41	43	43⅝	....	3/16	7/16
265	35¾	....	....	....	3/16	9/16
270	31	32⅜	....	....	¼	13/16
275	26⅛	27½	29	1/16	⅜	1⅛
280	21⅛	22½	24½	....	⅝	1⅝
285	16⅛	18¼	20½	1/16	1	2¼
290	11	13⅜	16⅝	1/16	1 9/16	3⅛
295	6	9⅝	12¾	1/16	2⅝	4½
300 ➤	1	6⅛	9⅝	1/16	4⅜	6¼
305	1/16	3½	6¾	4	7⅛	8½
310	....	1⅞	4⅝	....	10½	11⅞

Total call volume 202,438 Total call open int. 316,853
Total put volume 152,729 Total put open int. 552,232
The index: High 301.04; Low 297.65; Close 301.04, +3.39.

May 22, 1989

INDEX OPTIONS

Chicago Board

S&P 100 INDEX

Expire date Strike price	Sales	Open Int.	Week's High	Low	Price	Net Chg.	N.Y. Close
SP100 May280 p	13570	39975	⅛	1-16	1-16−	⅛	301.04
SP100 May285.	33844	13348	16⅛	9	16⅛+	7	301.04
SP100 May285 p	29793	49157	5-16	1-16	1-16−5-16		301.04
SP100 May290.	101701	22727	11⅛	4⅜	11	+ 6¼	301.04
SP100 May290 p	66060	35810	1 1-16	1-16	1-16−1 1-16		301.04
SP100 May295.	194761	35574	6¼	1 7-16	6	+ 4⅜	301.04
SP100 May295 p	96061	22569	3⅛	1-16	1-16−2 13-16		301.04
SP100 May300.	139666	31900	1⅝	¼	1	+ ⅝	301.04
SP100 May300 p	55637	5189	7	1⁻	1-16−6 15-16		301.04
SP100 May305..	26831	17678	¼	1⁻.	1-16−1-16		301.04
SP100 May305 p	453	69	10½	3⅞	1	− 16½	301.04
SP100 Jun260..	1604	3468	43	36⅝	4	+ 8⅜	301.04
SP100 Jun260 p	6055	12198	¼	⅛	3-16−1-16		301.04
SP100 Jun265..	450	698	34¾	34	34¾+	12	301.04
SP100 Jun265 p	1471	4718	⅜	⅛	3-16−3-16		301.04

20

The market improved, the S & P 100 Index improved, and by the time the last day of life for the Option was reached — Friday, May 19 (chart on the previous page) — the Index had closed at the *1* level.

In actual fact, intra-day speculative excitement had pushed the May 300 Call Index Option *higher* than 1 during the last few days of trading, in the hope that even on one day, a strong market might multiply the Option on the upside. (This happens quite easily!)

So the excerpt from **Barron's** for the weekly high-low-close shows (arrow) the May 300 Call Index Option selling at *1-5/8.*

In any event, we regard the "1/16 to 1" Index Option move as the foundation for the highly-promising "Pyramiding" concept, as we have just explained it. And later pages will expand on these ideas.

CURRENT SUPPLEMENT AVAILABLE

As this book was going to press, important developments were taking place. Long-Term *Warrants* on dozens of the most important Japanese companies, already trading in Europe, will, before too long, trade in the United States as well.

Stock Index *Futures* and Stock Index *Options* on the Japanese stock markets are already trading in Japan and elsewhere, and are preparing to trade in the United States. They will be highly-important speculative mediums, along the lines set forth in this book.

In the **Current Supplement,** the latest approaches to Index Option speculation are described, in light of the most recent stock market action.

In addition, the Current Supplement contains a valuable alphabetical listing by *Industry Group*, of all Warrants, Convertibles and Scores trading today, plus other current information important in today's market, regarding these fields.

The publishers of this book would like to send you this Current Supplement. Just send your name and address to:

Current Supplement, Department 96
R.H.M. Press
172 Forest Avenue
Glen Cove, New York 11542

There is no cost or obligation.

A Pause For Some Crucial Understanding Of "Futures-Related Program Trading"

Success with Index Option speculation has a great deal to do with "Futures-Related Program Trading," which serves to *accelerate* moves of the market as a whole. And such acceleration produces exaggerated short-term market moves which can take moderate Index Option profits and whirl them up to a highly-leveraged gain.

In order to understand this market phenomenon which has become of such importance in the past few years, there is a progression of factors which must be understood in turn.

First, there is the futures market, followed by Options on Stocks, followed by Index Futures and, finally, Index Options. If one understands these factors, it is much easier to see *why* Index Option speculation, when well-timed, and intelligently pursued, can be so successful.

Before we get back, then, to an in-depth analysis of the Index Option approaches we have presented in summary form, let us go over the above additional factors, each in turn.

Should the reader be impatient to get directly to Index Option strategies in order to aim at immediate profit opportunities in current markets, there is nothing wrong with turning to those later pages at this time. But we do advise such readers to also later *return* to the discussion which now follows, which can add greatly to an understanding of the entire speculative process with Index Options.

There is a direct line, in point of time and logical development, from *Commodity Futures* to *Options on Stocks*, to *Stock Index Futures* and, finally, to *Stock Index Options*, and understanding how they developed, one after the other, can itself make an important contribution to over-all understanding.

To begin with, *Commodities Futures* contracts are a very natural outgrowth of "risk-shifting" on the part of producers of the various commodities, the end users, and speculators. For example, a farmer with a soybean crop moving towards harvesting may be satisfied with the current market price for soybeans, and not wishing to take a chance on what the price might be after harvesting, *sells futures contracts*, which obligate the purchasers of the contracts to buy the farmer's soybeans at the stated price, at the stated time. The farmer has shifted the market risk from his shoulders to that of the buyers of the futures contracts.

Or a food producing company, being a heavy user of soybeans for their products, may *buy* such soybean futures contracts, locking in a specific price for delivery at a specific date, whereupon they can now know their production costs without being prey to the later whims of the marketplace.

The food-producing company has shifted its risk to the sellers of the soybean futures contracts. And getting between producers and end users, the commodity *speculators* take on most of that risk, some as buyers, some as sellers, or often a combination of both, in various hedging techniques, seeking a profit from the *price fluctuations* of the various commodities. To en-

FUTURES and OPTIONS

Season's High	Low		Week's High	Low	Close	Net Chg	Open Int.

Chicago Board of Trade

WHEAT
5,000 bu minimum; dollars per bushel

4.22	3.27	Jul	4.03	3.93	3.97½	+.03¼	22,836
4.29	3.50½	Sep	4.07¼	3.99¼	4.01	−.00½	21,106
4.40½	3.78	Dec	4.21	4.11	4.14½	−.01	20,335
4.43	4.03½	Mar	4.26½	4.15	4.18	−.03¼	6,232
4.32	3.98	May	4.14	4.03	4.07	−.02	1,289
3.85	3.65	Jul	3.76	3.70½	3.73	+.01	1,138

Fri. to Thurs. sales 71,316.
Total open interest 72,936.

CORN
5,000 bu minimum; dollars per bushel

3.60	2.33	Jul	2.72¾	2.60½	2.62	−.00¾	43,628
3.17¾	2.34¾	Sep	2.61	2.49½	2.51½	+.01¼	24,901
2.95	2.30¾	Dec	2.59	2.46¼	2.49	+.02¼	68,951
2.86½	2.38½	Mar	2.65½	2.53½	2.55¾	+.01¼	11,033
2.89½	2.43½	May	2.68¾	2.57¾	2.57¾	−.00¾	2,898
2.84	2.44½	Jul	2.69	2.57¾	2.57¾	−.01¼	1,756
2.57	2.34	Sep	2.57	2.50	2.51	+.04	73
2.52¼	2.31½	Dec	2.52¼	2.42	2.42½	+.00¼	1,342

Fri. to Thurs. sales 239,237.
Total open interest 154,582.

OATS
5,000 bu minimum; dollars per bushel

2.77	1.51	Jul	1.74½	1.51	1.52½	−.12	3,327
2.43	1.59¼	Sep	1.82	1.59¼	1.60	−.12	3,852
2.47	1.69	Dec	1.92	1.69	1.70	−.12	2,618
2.24	1.78¾	Mar	1.99½	1.78¾	1.78¾	−.11¼	310
2.01	1.86	May	2.01	1.88½	1.84	−.10	53

Fri. to Thurs. sales 9,679.
Total open interest 10,160.

SOYBEANS
5,000 bu minimum; dollars per bushel

9.86	6.88¾	Jul	7.60	7.20	7.31	−.02	24,481
9.51	6.62	Aug	7.32	6.94	7.04¾	−.00¼	12,502
8.35	6.27	Sep	6.94½	6.53½	6.64	−.02¾	8,607
7.93	6.14	Nov	6.81	6.35	6.45½	−.06	40,770
7.67	6.24	Jan	6.88½	6.43½	6.50¾	−.08¾	4,139
7.74	6.35	Mar	6.95½	6.52	6.61	−.07½	2,203
7.78	6.41	May	7.00	6.58	6.65	−.09½	1,309
7.00	6.42	Jul	7.00	6.58	6.65	−.10	554
6.48	6.48	Aug	.....	.....	6.51	−.12	1
6.30	6.30	Sep	.....	.....	6.39	−.06	1
6.60	6.15	Nov	6.45	6.28	6.29	−.06	104

Fri. to Thurs. sales 229,471.
Total open interest 94,671.

sure efficient trading to meet the needs of producers, end-users and speculators, the Commodities Futures market developed a marvelously-structured operation, allowing all concerned a wide variety of price/time choices.

To appreciate this, one need only look at the excerpt from **Barron's** weekly summary of the Commodity Futures market, on the preceding page, dated June 26, 1989. Note that for *Wheat*, each futures contract is for 5,000 bushels, and wheat for September delivery closed at 4.01, so the current market value of the contract is 5,000 x 4.01, or $20,050, with the buyer or seller of the contract having to put up about 10% in initial margin, or about $2,050 for each contract.

But more than that, note that there is a market for delivery in July, September and December in 1989, and March, May and July in 1990. Approximately the same is true for corn, oats and soybeans, and in each case there is also reported how many contracts were sold during the week and what the "Total open interest" was — meaning how many contracts were on the books.

The Commodity Futures market covers a very wide range of products, including the above-named, a long list of additional agricultural commodities, and cattle, coffee, orange juice, sugar, gold, silver, aluminum, copper, lumber, oil — and that is only a partial list.

In making possible all these vital markets, the various Commodities Exchanges *are not doing this as a public service*, but running this as a profit-making business, collecting their commissions from buyers and sellers alike, and smiling all the way to the bank. Consequently, the Exchanges are always on the lookout for *new products* to trade.

In 1973 came a brilliant idea, quite separate from commodities futures. What if one were to set up an efficient "secondary market" for *Options on Stocks?* There *was* an Option market for stocks prior to 1973, run by a group of "Put and Call Brokers" who arranged contracts to buy (Call Options) or sell (Put Options) on a relatively short list of stocks.

Each Option represented the right to buy or sell 100 shares of stock at a specific price for a specific period of time. Each such Option was "guaranteed" as to performance by a member firm of the New York Stock Exchange, and fees were charged throughout the process.

The major problem with such a personal, negotiated market was that once you entered into such an Option contract, if you wanted to get out of it, it was difficult and costly to sell the contract to another party. Therefore, typically, the holder of the contract would have to stay with his investment in the Option until expiration, or until profitable exercise.

In other words, there was no efficient *secondary market* where the Option contracts could be bought and sold at will. All that changed in April 1973 when the Chicago Board Options Exchange (CBOE) opened for business with standardized option terms for a long list of active stocks, creating a highly liquid secondary market, and also creating a bonanza for the Chicago Board Options Exchange as investors and professionals alike rushed in to participate in this new market.

Very soon the American Stock Exchange got into the

act, trading Options on another list of stocks, in the same manner, to be followed by the Philadelphia Stock Exchange, and other Exchanges.

Once again, an excerpt from the daily trading tables — this time from the **Wall Street Journal** — informs us immediately about the attractions of the new methods of trading Put & Call Options on stocks. Prior to the establishment of the Exchange-traded Options markets,

THE WALL STREET JOURNAL

FRIDAY, JULY 7, 1989

Option & NY Close	Strike Price	Calls – Last			Puts – Last		
		Jul	Aug	Oct	Jul	Aug	Oct
I B M	105	7³⁄₈	8	10	¹⁄₈	¹³⁄₁₆	1⁹⁄₁₆
111¾	110	3	4⅛	6¾	¹³⁄₁₆	2⅛	3⅛
111¾	115	¹¹⁄₁₆	1¹³⁄₁₆	4¼	3½	4⅞	5¾
111¾	120	⅛	⅝	2⅜	8¼	r	9¼
111¾	125	¹⁄₁₆	s	1¼	12¾	s	r
111¾	130	r	s	¹¹⁄₁₆	r	s	r
In Min	40	r	r	4⅜	r	r	r
42½	45	r	¾	1¼	r	r	r
In Pap	45	1⁷⁄₁₆	r	3⅛	⅜	1	1½
45⅞	50	¹⁄₁₆	¼	¹⁵⁄₁₆	4	r	r
45⅞	55	¹⁄₁₆	r	r	r	r	9
Itel	22½	¾	r	r	r	r	r
John J	40	8¾	s	s	r	s	s
49	42½	6¾	s	r	r	s	r
49	45	4⅛	s	6	⅛	s	1¹⁄₁₆
49	47½	2¼	s	4⅛	½	s	r
49	50	¾	1⁹⁄₁₆	2¾	1¾	2⅜	r
49	55	¼	½	1⅜	r	r	r

if you felt that the market was due for a goodly rise, and that IBM, as a market "bellwether," would certainly share in that rise, you had one thing you could do — you could buy IBM common stock.

If it was selling at, say, 111-3/4, you could invest $11,175 in 100 shares. If IBM did subsequently rise to, say, 125, you would have a $1,325 profit on your $11,175 investment. If, instead, IBM went *down* to, say, 100, you would have an $1,117 loss.

With the advent of Exchange-traded Options on stocks, a whole new world opened up for the trader looking for such a move. Now, if you were looking for a short-term rise in IBM, you could *buy a Call Option*, and even further, you would be able to choose from a *number* of Call Options, each expressing your expectations for IBM in a different dimension.

Thus, suppose you purchased one July 110 Call Option at 3 for $300 — the actual price shown on the table. With IBM common already at 111-3/4, the 110 Call was enjoying 1-3/4 points of value, so it was "in the money."

If IBM common then went up to *125* prior to the July expiration date for the Call Option, that Call, representing the right to buy at *110*, had a minimum value of 125 minus 110, or *15 points*. The Call would now be worth $1,500, and since you had paid $300 for the Call, your investment would have appreciated by $1,200, or *300%*. In contrast, 100 shares of IBM common, moving from 111-3/4 to 125, with $11,175 becoming worth $12,500, would show a gain of only *12%*.

This 12% gain for the common contrasts with the

300% gain for the 110 Call Option, so the *leverage* of a successful move with a listed Option on stocks is quite clear.

The leverage potential of an *out of the money* Call Option — therefore, a lower-price Call Option — can be quickly demonstrated. Suppose that, instead of buying the July 110 Call Option, you had purchased the July *115* Call, selling at 11/16 (68 cents).

The table gives us that price. With the common at 125, the 110 Call would have an intrinsic value of 125 minus 110, or *15 points*, making the 100 Calls worth $1,500, and representing a *1,354%* gain, as against the 12% gain for IBM common stock.

Of course, if you felt that the general market was going to *fall*, and that IBM would doubtless follow the market to the downside, you could buy a *Put* Option from the last 3 columns in the table.

(The first three columns quote July, August and October *Calls*, the next three columns quote July, August and October *Puts*.) We could go through exactly the same numbers as with the Calls, except that IBM common would be going *down* in price, and the out of the money Put Options — the "Strike Price" *higher* than IBM's price — would show the greatest percentage advance.

There is much to say about Exchange-traded Options on stocks, but at this time we are simply making the point that when the Chicago Board went from its Commodity Futures business to adding Options on stocks, it *vastly* increased its business, and a flood of commissions rewarded all the Exchanges that entered this business, from investors delighted to have this additional means of expressing their opinions about where individual stocks were headed, and the many potentially rewarding trading approaches that could be used with this new speculative market instrument.

Stock Index Futures

The Commodity Exchanges having scored such a great success by moving in on the securities business in stocks via Exchange-traded *Options on Stocks*, fertile minds kept thinking about further ways to augment commission business in the same area, and some time around 1978-1979, the idea was promulgated that one could trade *Futures contracts on stock Averages* or *"Indexes."*

This created a furor in the regulatory agencies for both the commodity markets and the securities markets, and resulted in literally years of hearings under the auspices of the Commodity Futures Trading Commission.

The first and obvious question was: since a stock market Index is assumed to be the "commodity" underlying the Futures contract, how do you make delivery? How do you "deliver" a market "Average"?

This proved to be not such a weighty argument because the vast majority of Commodity Futures contracts are never exercised. The Futures contracts are traded back and forth between speculators and hedgers and never result in any cotton or wheat or aluminum being "delivered," a "round turn" (a buy and a sell — or a sell and a buy) with a Commodity Futures extinguishing the contract. The Commodity Exchanges, pushing the idea of trading in Stock Index Futures, came up with the quite logical idea that the contracts that were still open when the moment of expiration came close, and premiums over exercise value went to 0, *would be settled in cash at the close of trading on the expiration day.*

That was simple to do, because at the termination of a contract, the "cash" or market price, and the Futures price *must converge.* (This fact is very important for understanding "Futures-Related Program Trading," which we will discuss in later paragraphs, and which serves to *accelerate* market moves, adding greatly to the "success ratio" in Index Option speculation.)

To show that convergence *must* happen, suppose, for example, that corn is selling at $2.00 a bushel in the cash market — that day's price for immediate action — and an expiring Futures contract on corn is selling at $2.10. An arbitrageur will sell Futures at $2.10 and buy corn at $2.00 in the cash market to make delivery, making a certain 10 cents a bushel.

The same thing would happen if expiring Futures were available at $1.90 per bushel when the cash market was $2.00. Here the arbitrageur would *buy* Futures at $1.90 per bushel and sell corn at $2.00 per bushel in the cash market. He would then demand delivery under his Futures contract and be ahead the same 10 cents per bushel.

This is theoretical conjecturing because there are too many experienced heads always looking at the Futures and cash markets, and what we have just described could never happen. The day a Futures contract is expiring, the Futures price and the cash price must be the same; they *"converge."*

We demonstrated this concretely in a report in the **R.H.M. Survey** in June 1986 with the Stock Index tables for June Futures expiring on June 20, 1986. The way such tables are currently presented, they are not as clear as the 1986 example, so we again utilize the table as shown (courtesy of the **New York Times**).

For each of the June Futures, look at the "Last Index" price, and then at the "settle" price, which is the last number on each line. What one sees is 240.71 for the close for the Value Line Stock Index for June, and 240.71 for the closing Index price. For the S & P 500 Stock Index, the June Future settles at 247.50, while the Index ends at 247.52. For the N.Y.S.E. Composite Index, the settle price for the June Future is 141.65, while the Index Price ends at 141.65 as well. And, finally, for the Major Market Index, the June Future settles at 358.73 and the Index Price ends the same way at 358.73.

The visual evidence tells us what we know as logical fact in any case — that on the day an Index Future expires, the Index price is exactly equal to the Future price.

Now we get on with the concept of "settlement will be made in cash," and the need for this is obvious, once you give it some thought. Suppose you had purchased that June Future on the S & P 500 some weeks back at 230.00, and here it is expiring at 247.50. Since the value of one contract for the S & P 500 Index is 500 times the

THE NEW YORK TIMES,

SATURDAY, JUNE 21, 1986

STOCK INDEXES

VALUE LINE STOCK INDEX (KCBT)
$500 X index number

248.80	197.00	Jun	241.80	239.10	240.71	−.39	7,081
250.35	200.05	Sep	244.60	242.00	243.60	+1.45	7,629
258.00	220.50	Dec	245.00	244.00	245.00	+1.50	108
253.20	238.80	Mar	246.25	246.25	246.25	+1.50	86

Last index 240.71, off 1.72.
Thu.'s sales 4,830.
Thu.'s open int 14,904, up 2.

S.&P. 500 STOCK INDEX (CME)
$500 x index number

250.40	183.90	Jun	247.70	243.65	247.50	+3.65	34,873
252.70	187.00	Sep	248.15	245.35	247.90	+2.40	70,689
254.60	178.40	Dec	250.20	247.50	249.90	+2.60	1,595
257.00	235.00	Mar	....	....	251.90	+2.50	18

Last index 247.52, up 3.46.
Thu.'s sales 86,075.
Thu.'s open int 107,175, up 476.

N.Y.S.E. COMPOSITE INDEX (NYFE)
$500 X index number

143.95	106.90	Jun	141.65	139.95	141.65	+1.60	5,344
145.40	108.10	Sep	142.45	141.00	142.30	+1.25	7,679
146.55	121.10	Dec	143.45	143.45	143.40	+1.35	1,002
147.70	136.90	Mar	143.50	143.50	144.50	+1.45	244

Last index 141.65, up 1.45.
Est. sales 11,469. Thu.'s sales 12,588.
Thu.'s open int 14,269, off 1,031.

MAJOR MARKET INDEX (CBT)
$250 x index number

359.25	310.90	Jun	359.00	353.10	358.73	+4.18	4,242
360.50	332.60	Jul	359.90	354.20	359.45	+3.70	1,186
360.50	338.70	Aug	359.50	355.00	359.50	+3.20	15
362.10	331.00	Sep	361.00	355.90	361.00	+3.80	127

Last index 358.73, up 4.25.
Thu.'s sales 8,630.
Thu.'s open int 5,570, up 3.

Index Number, the purchase made at *230* meant the contract was worth 500 x 230 or *$115,000*. Now, at expiration, the Index is at 247.50, so the contract is worth 500 x 247.50 or *$123,750*. The difference is $8,750 for each contract, and that is the profit. But who gives the purchaser the $8,750?

The answer is that when a Futures contract one has purchased, profits by $8,750, that amount is credited to one's account by the clearinghouse member with whom one has an account.

Settling in cash is a *highly efficient mechanism*, so its usefulness carried over to the next, and most successful, product conceived by the enterprising Exchanges that started from their "Commodities" base. That next product is "Index Options," which we will be discussing shortly.

The matter of how to "settle" Stock Index Futures upon expiration — it would be accomplished in cash — and other objections having been proved insubstantial during the hearings, the green light was finally given for trading, about four years after it was first proposed by the Kansas City Board of Trade. On February 24, 1982, trading commenced on the Futures for the Value Line Composite Index, and on April 20, 1982, trading commenced on the Chicago Mercantile Exchange for a Stock Index Futures contract based on the Standard & Poor's 500 Stock Index, to be followed in a few weeks by a Futures contract on the New York Stock Exchange Composite Index, to be traded on the New York Futures Exchange. The roster was completed at a considerably later date by Futures trading commencing on the Major Market Index.

The Crucial Difference Between Stock Index FUTURES, and Stock Index OPTIONS.

We are about to discuss Futures-Related Program Trading, and how its "acceleration" effect works its magic on Index Option speculation. But before we do that, let us fully comprehend one of the chief characteristics of Stock Index *Futures*, which is that potential gain and loss are *both* without limit.

And later we will assess the significance of the fact that for Index *Options*, gain is without limit, but chance of loss is *strictly* limited.

It is March 10, 1989, and on the Chicago Mercantile Exchange, the S & P 500 Index has closd at 292.88, while the June Future for the S & P 500 Index has closed at 297.65. We multiply this Futures price (297.65) by the multiplier for this Future (500) and come up with a value of *$148,825* for the Future.

Assume a buyer of 1 Future, and also assume he must have initial margin of about 10% of the $148,825 value, or about $14,882. If the market will fall, the Future will decline in price, and the buyer will be called upon to post *additional* margin to maintain the position.

The excerpt from the trading tables from **Barron's** for 3-13-89 shows that the greatest trading activity has been in March and June Futures (volume in the last column), and the figure in the last column where price is concerned, tells us where the June Future closed. The

March 13, 1989

Chicago Mercantile Exchange

S&P 500

points and cents

302.65	253.90	Mar	296.65	291.50	294.00	+2.05	54,380
306.15	263.80	Jun	300.40	295.10	297.65	+2.00	83,420
309.10	271.50	Sep	304.50	299.50	301.80	+2.35	935
311.80	298.90	Dec	307.85	304.30	306.45	+2.60	21

Last index 292.88, up 1.70.
Fri. to Thurs. sales 275,338.
Total open interest 138,756.

June 12, 1989

Chicago Mercantile Exchange

S&P 500

points and cents

328.45	263.80	Jun	328.45	321.65	327.70	+1.15	77,692
332.95	271.50	Sep	332.95	326.15	332.20	+1.15	66,662
336.45	298.90	Dec	336.45	330.20	336.20	+1.05	2,927
340.65	331.00	Mar	340.65	335.50	340.40	+.70	1

Last index 326.69, up 1.17.
Fri. to Thurs. sales 299,315.
Total open interest 147,282.

stock market advances over the next three months, and the close on June 9, 1989, from **Barron's** for June 12, finds the S & P 500 Index at *326.69*, a significant advance from the *292.88* which obtained on March 10th. The June Future will expire shortly, so we expect it to be selling not far from the Index price. This is indeed the case, with the Future closing at *327.70*.

The buyer of one Future on March 10th has a fine profit and decides to sell at 327.70. We multiply this figure by 500 and get $163,850. Since the value was *$148,825* when the purchase had been made, the profit is the difference between the two figures, or $15,025, and his brokerage account is credited with that amount.

Now we move to a more tumultuous time, in 1987. **Barron's** for August 3, 1987 gives us the close for the previous week's trading in Futures, and with the S & P 500 Index closing at *318.66*, the December Future has closed at *322.80*. Once again, a buyer has purchased 1 Future, the value of which is 500 x 322.80 or *$161,400*.

We will assume the buyer has put up 10% initial margin, or $16,140. We move to a sharply declining October 1987 (although still before the October 19th market crash), and for the week ending October 16th (again, courtesy of **Barron's**) we find that the December Future for the S & P 500 Index has closed at *282.25*. We multiply this figure by 500 to get its value, which is *$141,125*. If the Future is sold at this point, the loss is the difference between $161,400 and $141,125, or *$20,275*, and the buyer's brokerage account is debited by that amount.

Take careful note of the fact that for *both* examples

August 3, 1987

Chicago Mercantile Exchange

S&P 500

points and cents
320.30	229.90	Sep	320.30	309.20	320.20	+9.90	107,627
322.90	243.20	Dec	322.90	311.75	322.80	+9.90	8,835
325.25	281.00	Mar	325.25	314.20	325.25	+10.05	271
326.00	309.50	Jun	326.00	318.40	327.60	+9.95	32

Last index 318.66, up 9.39.
Fri. to Thurs. sales 305,493.
Total open interest 116,765.
S&P OTC 250 INDEX
points and cents
No open contracts.

October 19, 1987

Season's			Week's			Net	Open
High	Low		High	Low	Close	Chg	Int.

Chicago Mercantile Exchange

S&P 500

points and cents
342.35	243.20	Dec	317.00	277.00	282.25	−29.95	124,798
343.75	280.40	Mar	320.55	280.40	285.45	−30.35	8,365
345.90	284.20	Jun	322.65	284.20	286.00	−32.50	493
341.60	287.00	Sep	327.00	287.00	299.50	−22.25	40

Last index 282.94, off 28.11.
Fri. to Thurs. sales 465,290.
Total open interest 133,696.

of the purchase of Futures, there was *no limit* to the possible profit or loss. If, prior to the expiration date, the market had gone up and up and up, the *profit* for the Future would have taken a similar path. And if the market had gone down and down and down, the *loss* would have mounted with incessant margin calls along the way to "mark" the position "to market."

So buying a Future involves *both* the *unlimited* potential for gain, and *unlimited* potential for loss.

The Stock Index OPTION is Quite Different!

Look at the Index Options table for the close on Monday, July 10, 1989, and observe the very *wide* range of choices. The first three columns are *Call* Index Options, where one can profit if the S & P 100 Index (which parallels the movement of the market in the same manner that the Dow Jones Industrials do, and the S & P 500 Index does) moves *higher*.

The last three columns are *Put* Index Options, where one can profit if the S & P 100 Index moves *lower*. In the case of Calls, the Index must move higher than the Strike Price of the individual Option to see the Option develop a profit. And the greater the move of the Index above the Strike Price, the greater is the profit of the Call Option. Similarly, but in reverse, the Index must move *below* the Strike Price to see the individual Put Option develop a profit. One paramount point is this: In the dozens of choices which are available for

OPTIONS

Monday, July 10, 1989

Chicago Board

S&P 100 INDEX

Strike Price	Calls—Last Jul	Aug	Sep	Puts—Last Jul	Aug	Sep
260	42½	....	....	1/16	¼	....
265	....	....	....	1/16	⅜	....
270	32½	33	....	1/16	½	....
275	28½	....	....	⅛	⅝	1½
280	23	24¼	26½	⅛	15/16	2⅛
285	17¾	19¼	22	¼	1 7/16	2⅞
290	13¾	16	17⅝	½	2	3⅝
295	9⅛	12	14¾	⅞	3⅛	5
300	5	8½	11	2	4⅞	6⅝
305	2⅛	5½	8⅛	4⅜	7⅜	8¾
310	11/16	3⅜	5½	8¼	10⅜	12⅛
315	¼	2	3⅝	14	15	....
320	1/16	1	2½	....	....	....

Total call volume 85,887 Total call open int. 316,563
Total put volume 90,718 Total put open int. 427,333
The index: High 302.88; Low 300.79; Close 302.88, +2.09

speculation, among the rows of Calls and the rows of Puts, one all-important point must be recognized: where the purchase of a ***Future*** represents ***unlimited risk***, the purchase of any Index Option represents risk which is ***strictly limited*** to the initial cost of the Index Option. The potential for ***gain*** is unlimited, but the limit of ***loss*** is what one paid for the Option, and not a penny more. That this is the *basis* for successful speculation with Index Options, will be seen in the later in-depth discussions of the roads to such successes.

Futures-Related Program Trading

Industrial Shares Leap 29.88 Points On Heavy Futures-Related Trades

The above headline (courtesy of the **Wall Street Journal**) is typical of many such reported events, and is yet *on a small scale* compared to what has happened in past years, and will doubtless be happening again, as such Program Trading sees market moves of 40, 60 and even 80 points, as measured by the Dow Jones Industrial Average, erupt in either direction, depending on whether bullish or bearish trends gain quick strength.

As we will be demonstrating in these paragraphs, Program Trading *accelerates* market moves, causing a market rise to push even higher, and a market decline to push even lower.

This is of obvious large importance to Index Option positions, because such moves can whirl an Option selling at 1/16 up to the 1 mark quite easily, causing $625 to become worth $10,000 in a hurry.

When we deal in detail, in later pages, with the concept of "Pyramiding With Index Options," the part that a reinforced market move through Program Trading will play in a sought-for "success" will become very apparent. In following up on the above headline, the **Wall**

Street Journal 4-28-89 reported the following: "Initially, the Dow Average moved ahead only slightly. But around 10:30 a.m. EDT, *stock index futures took off and began trading at prices sharply higher than the indexes themselves.* Traders said the result was index-arbitrage trades that involve the rapid computer-driven program *selling of futures* and the *program purchase of baskets of stock.* Index arbitrage dropped off last year amid post-crash public criticism of the wild price swings to which it can contribute, but firms have beefed up operations again." (Emphasis added.)

And the **New York Times** 4-28-89: "With its inflation worries subsiding, the bond market rallied strongly yesterday, with prices rising and yields falling. Since lower interest rates on competing bonds are normally good for the stock market, the bond rally set off a simultaneous reaction in Chicago, where stock index futures are traded. Those futures, which are based on leading stock indexes like the Standard & Poor's 100-and-500-stock index, *surged, creating large price disparities between the futures contracts and the actual cash indexes.* Such large disparities breed index arbitrage or program trading. And analysts said such program trading, in which large institutional investors and brokerage firms *lock in profits by selling inflated futures contracts and buying huge baskets of stocks* that are intended as proxies for the cash indexes, played a large role in yesterday's rally." (Emphasis added.)

The key to understanding "program trading," as it was

spelled out above, is this: When index *Futures* sell at a premium above the immediate Index price, the arbitrageurs can lock in a riskless profit by selling the Futures short and buying the underlying stock.

At the settlement date of the Futures contract, the premium must disappear as Future price and Index price *converge.* Since the seller was *short* the Future at a premium above the Index price, the seller captures that premium.

And up until the settlement date, movement in the Future and the underlying stocks, where the arbitrage position is concerned, *will cancel each other out* so there will be no net gain or loss possible in that area and, therefore, *no risk.*

On the last day for the Future, the arbitrageur *must* earn his profit — and all this without any risk. Is it any wonder that Futures-Related Program Trading is now an inevitable part of the securities markets?

Exactly the same is true, in reverse, when a wave of *pessimism* hits the marketplace and Index futures sell at *a discount* to the Index price. Here, the arbitrageurs will *buy* the Futures and *sell* the underlying stocks to capture the discount at that same zero risk. For when settlement date of the Future arrives, the discount must *disappear,* again as Future price and Index price *converge.*

Index Futures develop a *premium* when investors

become very bullish on the market and expect the market to be selling much higher when settlement date of the Future arrives.

Since the action of the arbitrageur in this case is to sell the Future short and *buy the underlying stocks*, this additional buying (and it is done in huge quantities in a short period of time) *further* propels the market higher and *reinforces the bullishness* of the investor.

More buying comes into the Index Futures and *the premium over the Index price goes still higher,* precipitating *more* arbitrage activity in selling Futures and buying stocks. The entire action *feeds on itself*, pushing stocks sharply higher.

This is obviously a rewarding sequence of events for anyone owning Call Index Options.

What we have just described is completely true as well on the *down*side, where arbitrageurs keep *selling* stocks as they are buying Futures, reinforcing the bearish feelings of investors whose bearishness is causing Index Futures to sell at a discount.

The action feeds on itself on the *downside*, pushing stocks lower and lower. And, once again, anyone owning *Put* Index Options is greatly helped by these developments.

Complaints may be heard about the effects of Futures-Related Program Trading on market movement, but there is no way to stop Index arbitrage as long as Index Futures trade and *must* sell at either a premium or a discount to the Index price, reflecting bullishness or bearishness of investors. Index Arbitrage is now an inescapable part of the financial scene.

The Effect Of Program Trading On Index Option Speculation

When Futures-Related Program Trading gets *really* going (at this writing there is still only a modest imitation of what will surely'come in later markets) there will be wide market swings.

For example, as the market is propelled to the *up*side, Index *Put* Options move lower and lower in price. If one is successful in timing a *reversal,* the market will turn around and head sharply to the downside, causing the Put Option to rise equally sharply in price.

Exactly the same thing happens in reverse when the market is being propelled to the *down*side. Index *Call* Options will move lower and lower in price as the market declines, and if a purchase is followed by that same *reversal* — this time to the *up*side — a large profit will ensue.

Program Trading plays a large part in this entire process, *accelerating* market moves both to the upside and the downside, which very often leads to a reversal when securities prices have been "stretched" too far in one direction.

This then becomes a perfect market environment for Index Option speculation as we have just described it since the purchases subscribers will make are at very low prices (from 1/2 down to 1/16), while the gains range from large to spectacular. This means that 3, 4 and 5 *failures* — all constituting *small* losses — will easily be outweighed by one success, since a typically *very* large gain results.

The Potentially Momentous Effects on American Markets of Trading In Stock Index Futures On The Japanese Market

The Japanese stock markets are tightly controlled by the government. Indeed, some observers have gone so far as to say those markets are "rigged" in many important aspects. We tend to go along with that evaluation, but only up to a point, because markets are bigger than the authorities!

One factor is immediately significant, and that is that *short-selling is not allowed in Japan.* But, in late-1988, a development took place which we are certain the authorities did not welcome, but which they had no power to stop.

Trading began in stock index Futures on the Tokyo Stock Exchange, these Futures called TOPIX, while Nikkei Stock Average Futures began trading on the Osaka Stock Exchange.

In a full-page description of these new Futures, presented by one of the largest Japanese financial companies, Nikko, there was portrayed a valuable chart on Stock Index Futures in the United States, which we have reproduced on the next page to show the enormous in-

WARRANTS, OPTIONS and CONVERTIBLES

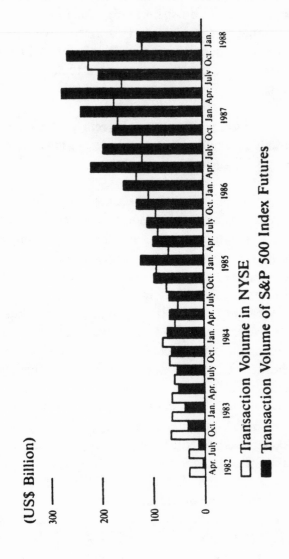

(US$ Billion)

☐ Transaction Volume in NYSE

■ Transaction Volume of S&P 500 Index Futures

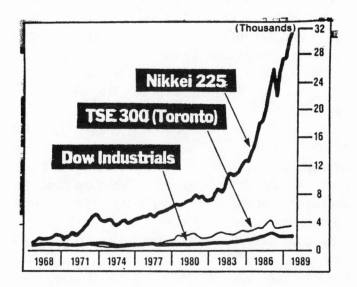

fluence of the S & P 500 Stock Index Futures, since the transaction volume of those Futures (the market value of Futures, as we have previously explained it) has outstripped the cash market on the New York Stock Exchange for most months since 1984.

Now it is expected that the new Stock Index Futures trading in Japan will move towards topping the value of stocks traded on the Tokyo Stock Exchange, and the "momentous" developments that could occur would be the build-up in *Futures-Related Program Trading* with both the Nikkei and TOPIX Stock Index Futures.

As we stated above, the Japanese authorities did not welcome these Stock Index Futures, but if they had *not*

49

started trading in Japan, they would have certainly begun trading in Chicago. So it undoubtedly was felt by Tokyo that the Index Futures would be safer to start trading in Japan, where the authorities could have *some* control. We view this, however, as a vain attempt to control the uncontrollable! Probably the object was to simply buy time.

Look at the chart shown for the Nikkei 225 Stock Average, on the preceding page, showing how that Average compares with the stocks in the Toronto Stock Exchange's 300 Stock Average, and the Dow Jones Industrial Average in the United States. (The chart is courtesy of **Barron's**.)

Since the date of the chart, the Nikkei has gone still higher, and what is now looming directly ahead? The **London Economist** for 1-21-89 had the following summary of expectations, which must be considered in light of the *huge* rise in Japanese equities:

"Financial-futures markets in Chicago have spent a year convincing American regulators that they did not cause the stock market crash of 1987. They had better start marshalling their arguments for the Japanese authorities that *they are not going to cause the crash of 1990.*

"Later this year, both the Chicago Board of Trade and the Chicago Mercantile Exchange are due to start trading contracts in Japanese stock-index futures, either directly or through Globex, the Merc's trading system . . . the huge trading volumes that are common in Chicago could *cause violent swings in the prices of the underlying stocks on the cash markets in Japan.*

"Some say that such volatility could induce a panicky bear market in the underlying cash dealing in Tokyo, or amplify one that has been caused for other reasons. Trading stock-index futures is the only way to short-sell the Tokyo market . . . " (Emphasis added.)

We feel it is inevitable that when a two-way street develops for Japanese stocks — for some years now (see chart) it has gone one way — up — Program Trading *will* start in force, and it could shake not only the Japanese markets, but world markets as well.

The increased volatility for this country's stock markets would have *large* meaning for Index Option speculation, as we have been describing it.

Learning From Some Index Option Events
Over Recent Years

In recounting a string of Index Option successes, covering a period of some years, let us deal immediately with an anticipated criticism: these are all *profitable* positions — what about the *losses*?

There definitely *were* losses — quite a number of them over the span of years covered. But, to begin with, the ratio of losses to successes was better than we had a right to expect and, in any case, if one would add up all the losses, they would not even remotely begin to approach the size of the profits generated by the successes. This will soon become very clear.

We are dealing here with the *cornerstone* of "Successful Index Option Speculation," that cornerstone being: keep commitments *small*. The word "small" is a relative word, and, of course, it means small in relation to the total amount of funds an individual feels he can devote to such a speculative endeavor. If this dictum is obeyed, the way is clear for a pronounced over-all success with Index Options.

The word "small" gives way to something else in "Pyramiding," where one utilizes a portion of the profits of a position to make a *larger* Index Option commitment, aiming at a leveraged profit, but using only profits rather than original capital. We will be explaining that in detail in later pages.

The successful positions we have chosen to describe

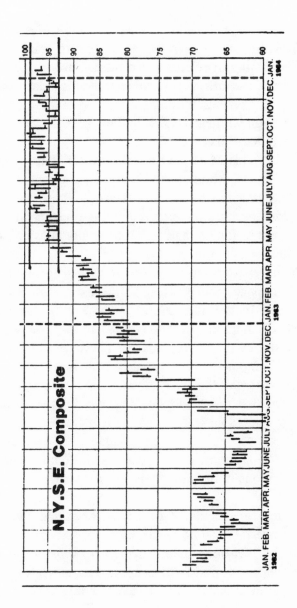

— all of them from the pages of past issues of the **R.H.M. Survey** — each has something to teach about the techniques of selection and timing, as well as other important features, which will enable the reader to seize *today's* Index Option opportunities.

We begin with early-1984, and an analysis we did for the **R.H.M. Survey** of February 3, 1984, which was headed: "This Market Can Fall Out Of Bed — And What To Do About It." The first paragraph began:

"This is a terrible looking market whose technical underpinnings are just barely holding together in some important instances, and which have already given way in other equally important instances."

In the chart of that period of time (shown on the previous page, and courtesy of the **New York Times**), presented in the January 20, 1984 Survey, we see a Trend Channel in effect May 1983 through December 1983, and by the Survey issue of February 3, 1984, the NYSE Composite Index was already at 94.32, very close to the bottom of the Trend Line, and we were expressing our view that the chances of a downside breakthrough were considerable.

In view of this, we were recommending purchase of Index *Put* Options, and we explained the attraction of such Options in that Survey issue, as follows:

"Prior to the advent of *Exchange-traded Put Options*, investors had no means by which to profit from a falling market other than to *sell stocks short*. (The old-style over-the-counter Put Options were much too complex and cumbersome for the average investor).

"Very few investors ever sold stocks short because of the unfamiliarity of such a procedure, and also because of the extreme tension involved in having *unlimited risk on the upside.*

"Meanwhile, buying Exchange-traded Put Options on individual stocks was an improvement over previous alternatives, but ran into the unquestioned truth of the proposition that *it is much more rewarding to apply the insights of Technical Analysis to the stock market as a whole, rather than to individual stocks.*

"With the advent of the *Index Option*, all this changed, and it is now just as possible to attempt to benefit from a falling market via Index *Put* Options, as it is to seek profits in a rising market by buying securities — the typical bent of the investor.

"One's *risk* in purchasing Index Put Options is the cost of the original purchase and not a cent more. But if there is a noticeable decline in the market, the Index Put Option can yield quite attractive percentage profits, while if there is a *substantial* drop in the market, those profits can be very large.

"Indeed, where selling a common stock short means limited chance of gain but unlimited potential for loss, buying an Index Put Option means strictly limited loss potential, but unlimited gain potential." (Original emphasis throughout.)

At that time, we were following the policy of the **R.H.M. Survey** itself, purchasing the recommended Options with R.H.M. funds, and then discussing the results of the purchases in the weekly issues of the Survey. By the issue of April 13, 1984, the results of the Put Index Option purchases were already in, and reported on in the following fashion:

"We come now to a discussion of what can be accomplished in a falling market with Put Index Options, when the market demonstrates the correctness of our choice by indeed slipping into a noticeable decline. As subscribers know, we have been giving 'practical demonstrations' to subscribers in the pages of the Survey by making actual investments with R.H.M. funds in different Index Options and reporting on them in our weekly issues.

"Since we were expressing a basic *bearishness* in the Surveys of January and February 1984, outlining what we viewed as technical deterioration in the status of the general market, it was natural that we were placing greatest emphasis on the purchase by R.H.M. of *Put* Index Options. Our negative feelings about the market reached a peak in the Survey of 2-3-84 with the heading: 'This Market Can Fall Out Of Bed — And What To Do About It.' The 'What To Do About It' portion referred to, of course, *the purchase of Put Index Options*, and we had been recommending such purchases for many weeks as we made our R.H.M. purchases."

At this point in the report, we reproduced the actual brokerage confirmations, which is not necessary to do in these pages.

"What is significant here is the *high-leverage* shown by very low-price, out of the money Put Index Options, when there is a pronounced move to the downside by the general market. Thus, in the first set of transactions, 20 *March 160 Puts* purchased at 9/16 for $1,125 were sold at 7-1/2 for $15,000 in about 5 weeks time! The *February 90 Puts*, having been purchased weeks earlier, had to content themselves with a comparatively moderate 80% gain. But the *April 155 Puts* had a very fast and very large gain, a $1,625 commitment in 20 Puts (at 13/16) being sold for $9,000 in little more than one week's time. Finally, the *March 90 Puts*, the lowest-priced and most 'out of the money' purchases scored a substantial success, a $3,187 purchase being sold for $19,500, mostly in a matter of weeks. Over-all: *$7,500 invested in these Put Index Options had been sold for $46,312* in that short period of time." (Original emphasis throughout.)

The above considerable gains were earned in a matter of weeks, and the basis for buying *Put* Index Options had been explained in previous Survey issues as being the extreme weakness in the Dow Jones Transportation Average, the savage slashing of prices for a number of individual stocks in the public eye stemming from minor diminution of earnings, the breaking of the Advance-Decline Line on the downside, and other negative technical events.

All this increased the potential for a downside break of the sideways Trend Channel shown on the previous page. "Technical Analysis of Stocks," which leads to "market timing," is one of the most important elements

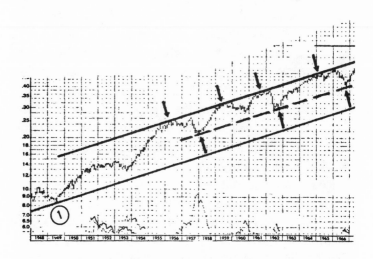

in putting the odds on one's side in selecting an Index Option commitment. *Trend Line Analysis*, for us, is the most important part of Technical Analysis, and is based on the *fact* that the market moves in cyclical patterns, greatly helping one to anticipate market turning points. To demonstrate the cyclicality, a chart of the N.Y.S.E. Composite Index, covering the period from 1948 to 1984, from the Survey of June 1, 1984, is presented in two sections. Note that from 1949 through 1973, *one* Trend Channel encompassed the entire market action, with the arrows pointing to market turning points, as upper and lower Trend Lines were touched. At the beginning of 1974, this Trend Channel was broken on the downside at (3), and a new Trend Channel held sway, the numbers on that part of the chart again indicating market *turning points*. What you are looking at

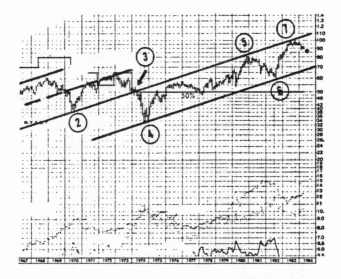

are two perfect Trend Channels, each perfectly parallel to the other one, with the Trend Lines involved all providing a multiplicity of "signals" for market turning points.

This "cyclicality" is very evident, not only in 35-year charts, such as the 1949-1984 portrayal in these two pages, but in charts covering a few years, and a few *weeks* too! One of the major points to remember is that *whenever* a Trend Line is being approached, there are *two* possibilities: (1) there will be a "bounce" away from the Trend Line, leading to a "reversal," or (2) there will be a *breakthrough* of a Trend Line, meaning a "new ballgame."

In either case, a "reversal" or a "breakthrough," a well-selected *Index Option* can profit *greatly* from an-

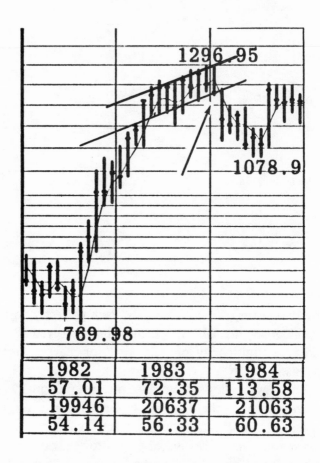

1982	1983	1984
57.01	72.35	113.58
19946	20637	21063
54.14	56.33	60.63

ticipating the move correctly. The chart above, excerpted from **Long Term Values** gives valuable insight into the role that can be played by a *short-term* chart. Note that most of 1983 was dominated by a modestly-uptilted Trend Channel. (In drawing Trend Lines, we connect the *closing* price, which is the horizontal tick, rather than the extremes of any one price line.)

There we have the Trend Channel with the first line in 1984 (January) closing directly at the lower Trend Line. As we have already pointed out, there is a whole array of negative factors very evident. The Transportation stocks have sagged badly and the Advance-Decline Line has broken on the downside, in its chart. (The Advance-Decline Line is an important technical indicator, which is the cumulative daily sum of the excess of stocks which have advanced against those that have declined.)

Further, it is a tried-and-true maxim that a market that greets good news in lackluster fashion, but over-reacts to what is viewed as bad news, is a market that is getting ready to move lower, and that was the case at the end of 1983.

The combination of those factors, and others not mentioned at this time, caused us to recommend Put Index Options in the pages of the Survey, and take those positions with R.H.M. funds. The result was an investment of *$7,500* becoming worth *$46,312* in a matter of weeks. And, of course, it was the the *chart*, as shown, which alerted us to the possibility of a downside break.

In light of the potentially lower markets to come, *another* role for very low-price, highly-leveraged Index Put Options moved into view. Here is what we wrote in the Survey of January 20, 1984:

"Turning to the March 90 *Put* Option, on the same New York Stock Exchange, it has virtually disappeared at the *1/8* mark, and subscribers worried about what a market spill to the downside might do to their portfolio could well consider the cheap insurance embodied in a purchase of these Put Options at 1/8, or $12.50 for each Option. March 16 is *two months away*, and no one can guarantee that the market will not be sharply lower by that time — in which case the highly-leveraged profits that those Put Options could show would make up for a good deal of the losses suffered by one's common stock holdings.''

That is exactly how the recommendation *did* work out. At the 1/8 low, $1,250 would have purchased 100 March 90 Put Options. For the week ending February 10, 1984, the March 90 Put Option sold at *2-1/8*, whereupon 100 Options were worth *$21,125*, which had been accomplished in about three week's time.

Such a gain (about $20,000) would have gone a long way towards offsetting losses that might have occurred in an individual's portfolio of stocks, and leads to a general conclusion: If you feel concern about the potential for a sharp downside move in the market, and what effect this would have on a list of stocks you are holding, buying some very low-price, out of the money, *Put* Index Options, can provide a fine "Hedge" against eventualities.

Thus, if your fears are proved incorrect, and the market moves *higher*, the investment in the Put Options will be lost, but the gain in your stocks will much more than make up for the small loss. On the other hand, if your fears are proved *correct*, and the market moves sharply to the downside, the profit in the Put Option position could offset most, or all, of the losses developing in the list of stocks.

CURRENT SUPPLEMENT AVAILABLE

As this book was going to press, important developments were taking place. Long-Term *Warrants* on dozens of the most important Japanese companies, already trading in Europe, will, before too long, trade in the United States as well.

Stock Index *Futures* and Stock Index *Options* on the Japanese stock markets are already trading in Japan and elsewhere, and are preparing to trade in the United States. They will be highly-important speculative mediums, along the lines set forth in this book.

In the **Current Supplement,** the latest approaches to Index Option speculation are described, in light of the most recent stock market action.

In addition, the Current Supplement contains a valuable alphabetical listing by *Industry Group*, of all Warrants, Convertibles and Scores trading today, plus other current information important in today's market, regarding these fields.

The publishers of this book would like to send you this Current Supplement. Just send your name and address to:

Current Supplement, Department 96
R.H.M. Press
172 Forest Avenue
Glen Cove, New York 11542

There is no cost or obligation.

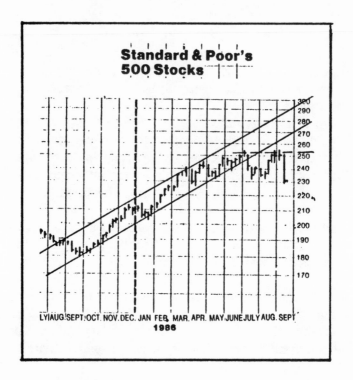

Standard & Poor's 500 Stocks

"Technical Analysis" Scores Again With Low-Price Index Options In 1986

Labor Day is always considered by this writer to be a time of potential market turbulence, and, therefore, gets special attention. This was particularly true in 1986 because of what the chart of the S & P 500 Stock Index (excerpted from the **New York Times**) tells us. Indeed, there are *several* important messages from this chart, which we shall be describing.

Once again the *validity* of Trend Line Analysis is demonstrated as an ascending Trend Channel encompasses all market action from September 1985 through June 1986.

A number of tops and bottoms throughout that period were useful at the time in anticipating, and utilizing for short-term trading, a market *reversal*, as the market "bounced" away from each Trend Line in turn.

But in July 1986, it did *not* "bounce." Rather it *broke through* the Trend Line and, as we stated on a previous page, this made the market a "new ball game," for at least *some* time to come. Now we come to another *highly* useful tenet of "Technical Analysis," which is the *"pullback."*

Very often, when a Trend Line is broken, the market turns around and retraces some, or even all, of the breakthrough, until it gets back to the broken Trend Line when — almost always — the market again continues in the direction of the original breakthrough. Such a "pullback" is *very* useful in timing the establishment of an Index Option position.

In this case, of course, we were looking for the market to move to the upside in that so typical action of a "pullback," and we were not disappointed, as shown by the August snapback towards the broken Trend Line.

However, this time the S & P 500 Index never made it all the way back to the Trend Line. Instead, it stopped at the early-July high, creating a "Double Top." Now, a Double Top itself is very often a precursor of *downside* action to come, so in the pages of the Survey at the time, we were recommending the purchase of Index *Put* Options as the "pullback" was under way. One of the welcome developments was the fact that as the market pushed to the upside in that August period, Put Options were getting *progressively cheaper*, which is the natural course of events. When the market is moving to the upside, *Puts* get cheaper and cheaper, while when the market is moving to the downside, *Calls* get cheaper and cheaper.

That is why we typically recommend "leaning against the wind," which is buying the Index Options that are getting cheaper and cheaper as the market moves the other way. We do this when there is a good expectation of a *reversal*, and if such does indeed take place, the substantial number of Options that have been, through Dollar Averaging, purchased at those cheaper prices become responsible for a *large* profit.

Once again, we were making purchases with R.H.M. funds, and reporting on those actions in the Survey, as the best means of projecting our ideas on Index Option speculation in the most concrete fashion. In the November 7, 1986 issue of the **R.H.M. Survey**, we reproduced the relevant brokerage confirmations and reported on the results, as follows:

On 8-20-86, we had purchased 50 October 205 Put Options for the S & P 100 Index at 1/4, costing $1,250.

(We are ignoring commissions in all of these discussions, for purposes of clarity. The profits that accrue upon a successful position are typically of such dimensions that commission charges are not significant. We also ignore "pennies" in the calculations.)

On 8-25-86, we purchased an additional 50 October 205 Put Options at 3/16, costing $937.

Now comes another important guidepost for the reader. Whenever we are desirous of buying additional Options at a very low price, even though the market quotations at the time are *above* the price area we are aiming at, we do not hesitate to "stick in a bid." The reason for this is that we *are* willing to buy at that lower price, if it happens to sell down during market fluctuations, and — we have nothing to lose by making the bid.

In this case, there *were* the appropriate fluctuations, and we bought an additional 100 of the same October 205 Put Options at *1/16*, for *$625.*

Adding up the above purchases, we now had *200* October 205 Put Options, which had cost us a total of *$2,812.*

If the scale down prices at which the purchases were made varied somewhat from the 1/4, 1/8,1/16 typically utilized with "Dollar Averaging," it was because we felt strongly attracted to those Put Options, *expecting* a downside move for the market, and we took what we could get at the time.

If we had to pay 3/16 instead of 1/8, we simply paid

the 3/16. Most of the time, however, we do not vary from the scale of 1/4, 1/8, 1/16 in Dollar Averaging.

As seen on the chart, when the S & P 500 Stocks made its "Double Top," it bounced away rather violently to the downside, at which time it felt quite good to be owning *Put* Index Options.

Now, demonstrating the fact that when a quick and substantial profit is at hand (substantial in terms of the original investment), you should not hesitate to take those profits, on September 15, 1986, about three weeks after our purchases, we sold the 200 Put Options in two lots.

One lot was 100 Options at 13/16, and the second lot was 100 Options at 7/8. We took the profits because our analysis of the behavior of the market at the time did not lead us to expect that there would be a further *substantial* downside move.

100 Options at 13/16 comes to $8,125.

100 Options at 7/8 comes to $8,750.

The total received for the 200 Options was $16,875.

Our investment in 200 October 205 Put Index Options had seen *$2,812* become worth *$16,875* in about three weeks time. So, in this particular example, the reader has learned to be alert to an opportunity following the breakthrough of a Trend Line, via the "pullback," and to pay attention to the message of a "Double Top." Thus, the intimate relationship of *Technical Analysis* to Index Option speculation.

To make more emphatic the usefulness of the "pullback," and, consequently, one of the major reasons for watching Trend Lines, *whenever* a Trend Line is broken, there is always the strong possibility that the break will go a certain distance, and then turn around and head for the broken Trend Line.

At such a time there are some strong reasons for buying very low-price Index Options that are appropriate for this move. Thus, as we saw with the July 1986 break to the downside, followed by a pullback to the upside, *Put* Index Options were getting cheaper as the Index moved back up. Since, *very* often, a pullback is followed by the resumption of movement in the direction of the break (down, in this case), Put Options made sense, and *did* result in a fine profit.

Exactly the same procedure would be applicable to *Call* Options, where there is a breakthrough of an *upper* Trend Line, followed by a pullback, which is headed down, and ultimately followed by a continuation of upside movement.

Trend Line Analysis is one of the most important ingredients going into selection and timing of an Index Option commitment.

Reviewing Index Option Definitions

In previous pages we detailed how *Futures* operate, and the development of *Index Futures*, with heavy emphasis on "financial" Futures. In 1983 came another bold idea from the Chicago Board Options Exchange. In addition to Options on *stocks*, winning or losing from the movement of individual stocks, why not Options on the *market as a whole*, winning or losing from the movement of the entire market? These would be Options on a stock market "Average," or "Index."

Very quickly after trading commenced in Index Options, the *S & P 100 Stock Index*, known familiarly by its symbol — *OEX* — forged far ahead in popularity with traders, and has remained so to this day. Thus, as we write, for Friday, July 14, 1989, the S & P 100 Index traded 152,070 contracts in Call Options, and 203,334 contracts in Put Options, for a total of *355,404* contracts.

The S & P 100 is a *market-weighted* Index, meaning that the more shares of stock outstanding for an individual company in the Index, the greater will be the effect on the Index of movement in that stock. This means that General Motors, General Electric, IBM etc., count heavily in the fluctuations of this Index.

Coming next in activity is the *Major Market Index (XMI)*, trading on the American Stock Exchange, which is an *equally*-weighted Index, the movement in the stocks of smaller companies having as much influence as the larger companies, where movement in the Index is concerned.

Friday, July 14, 1989

OPTIONS

Chicago Board

S&P 100 INDEX

Strike Price	Calls—Last			Puts—Last		
	Jul	Aug	Sep	Jul	Aug	Sep
260	....	....	....	....	3/16	....
265	....	....	....	....	3/8	....
270	37¼	....	....	1/16	3/8	....
275	32¼	....	....	1/16	½	1 5/16
280	24	....	31	1/16	11/16	1 9/16
285	23	20¾	....	1/16	1 1/16	2⅛
290	17½	19⅜	18¾	⅛	1½	2 15/16
295	12¾	15¼	16¾	5/16	2 5/16	3⅞
300	7⅞	11⅛	13¾	⅝	3½	5⅛
305	3¾	7½	10½	1 11/16	5⅛	6¾
310	1 5/16	4¾	7½	4⅛	7¼	8¾
315	5/16	2⅞	5⅜	8⅝	10⅝	12½
320	1/16	1 7/16	3¼	....	15⅛	....

Total call volume 152,070 Total call open int. 321,716
Total put volume 203,334 Total put open int. 536,073
The index: High 307.28; Low 302.53; Close 307.18, +1.69

On the day in question, 21,004 Call contracts and 22,066 Put contracts were traded, for a total of *43,070* contracts. 355,404 contracts for the S & P 100 Index, against 43,070 contracts for the Major Market Index, and it is downhill after that for the other Indexes, so it is clear that the "action" is in the OEX.

While the much larger volume of trading on the OEX is highly desirable from the point of view of getting in and out of positions expeditiously, we do not completely ignore the other Indexes. Particularly with the *New York Stock Exchange Index*, which has a very modest trading volume, we sometimes find an attractively-priced (comparing that price proportionately, with the OEX price) Call or Put Option, and proceed to "stick in a bid," whereupon we are happy to get the Option at our price, or have lost nothing by making the attempt.

In the Index Option table shown on the preceding page for the close of trading on July 14, 1989 (courtesy of the **Wall Street Journal**), the whole array of Option choices is again shown, the first three columns being for *Call* Options, and the second three columns being for *Put* Options.

Three expiration months are always trading, and when the nearest month expires on the third Friday of its expiration month, Options for a new month begin trading.

One rule of thumb to keep in mind is that when an expiration Friday arrives and one month is finished, the *other two* expiration months *move over* one column in the tables. We have always found that Option premiums weaken in price as the time for changeover arrives, so if you are looking to make a purchase, that particular time could be advantageous.

Conversely, if you are thinking of selling an Option position, it may be best to do it before the "column changeover" takes place.

Options are priced at *100 times* the price shown. Thus, the August 310 Call in the table, shows up at 4-3/4 and 100 times 4.75 is *$475*, and that is the price of each Option, if you want to buy or sell. *10* Options would cost 10 x 475, or $4,750.

Each point on the Index represents a move of $100 in value per Option. Thus, if a July 300 Call is selling at 0 premium at *5*, because the Index is at *305*, if the Index would move up by 5 points to 310, the Option would *have* to go up 5 points as well, to sell at *10*. That would be an advance in value of $500 for each Option, and if you owned 10 Options, the gain would be *$5,000*.

That tells us why an Index Option will move sharply higher in price if the S & P 100 Index has a sharp move. *Calls* will move up sharply if the Index *rises* strongly, and *Puts* will move up sharply if the Index is weak.

Just as with Index Futures, contracts are *settled in cash* at expiration. And do not fear that if you fail to sell your Option on the last day, when it has exercise value, that you will lose your profit. Your Option will be valued at the closing price of the expiration day, and your account will be credited with that amount.

Of course, if you have sold an Option *short* and there is value in the Option on expiration day, your account will be *debited* in the same manner. And on any day *prior* to expiration day, you can, of course, buy or sell Index Options at the going market prices, as shown in the table.

Having completed our summary of Index Option definitions, let us now proceed to *remarkable* events with Index Options in 1987, and what lessons those happenings have for today's and tomorrow's "Opportunities With Index Options!"

The February 255 Call Index Options

We have already described the profits that accrued with the *October 205 Put Options* in August - September 1986, and that success shows up in the downtrend Channel visible on the chart (excerpted from **Long Term Values**). But stock market movement is an *ongoing* thing, and what was bearish after Labor Day in 1986, began turning bullish as the close of the year came into view

Thus, the upper Trend Line of the Trend Channel was pierced on the upside, although modestly, in November and December, and with other technical factors turning promising, we began to look for an Index Option commitment that would benefit from an anticipated turn to the upside in early-1987.

We settled on the *February 255 Call Index Option*, selling at *9/16* at the time, so that the Dollar Averaging approach would find the next purchase to be made at *1/4*, to be followed by *1/8* and *1/16*, if the Option got that low.

Note: In Dollar Averaging, we like to start at about the *1/2* level. But if we think quite well of the commitment and it is selling at 9/16, or even 5/8, we do not "quibble," but start at that level. However, whether the start is at 1/2, 9/16 or 5/8, the next purchase is almost always at *1/4*, to get back on a regular track, so that open orders can be placed.

Once the first purchase is made and we get into the

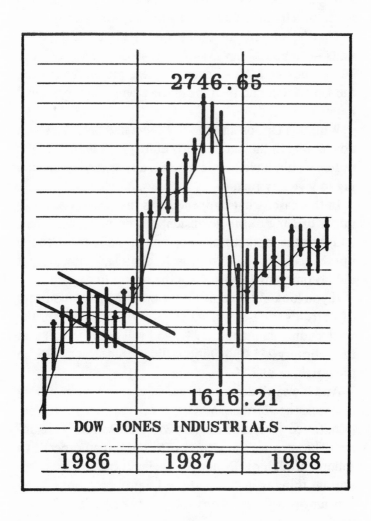

Dollar Averaging sequence, we have the advantage of giving our open orders to the broker, and then not having to watch market action any longer, for that purpose.

That is, we tell our brokers — if we are using $500 units — to buy 20 Options at 1/4, 40 Options at 1/8 and 80 Options at 1/16 — each of these purchases costing the same $500, and then the market determines what will happen.

With this Option situation, if there had been a sudden downswing in the market, it is quite possible that *all* the orders would have been executed, and without our having to give any further instructions.

In this case, what happened was that there was some minor drifting to the downside, but no more than that, and then the market picked up and began to move to the upside. *During* that "downside drifting," however, it did become possible to make the next purchase.

If you look at the table on the opposite page (courtesy of **Barron's** for 1-5-87), which gives the statistics for the week ending January 2, 1987, you will note (arrow) that the February 255 Call Options did indeed sell at 3/16, so the purchase at *1/4* was made.

And it was all done automatically, without our having to check the broker, or seek other means of information, to see what the February 255 Call Options were doing. This stresses the virtues of using "open orders" to follow through on Dollar Averaging. And the most important thing is that you are certain of executions when it is an open order, when the price reaches the desired level.

January 5, 1987
BARRON'S
Chicago Board

S&P 100 INDEX

Expire date Strike price	Open Sales	Week's Int.	High	Low	Net Price	Chg.	Close
SP100 Feb215 p	4029	9102	⅝	¼	¼ −	⅛	235.18
S~~...~~			16¾		⅝ −		18
SP100 Feb220 p	12342	182...	½	11-16	13 −	-16	235.18
SP100 Feb225 ..	820	1808	13	9	12¾ −	¾	235.18
SP100 Feb225 p	12739	18366	3⅛	1⅝	1¾ +	1-16	235.18
SP100 Feb230 ..	3605	5689	9⅛	5¾	8¾ −	1	235.18
SP100 Feb230 p	12070	17848	5¼	3	3⅛	......	235.18
SP100 Feb235 ..	11045	11231	6⅜	3½	5¾ −	⅞	235.18
SP100 Feb235 p	5616	6904	8¼	4⅞	5¼ +	⅛	235.18
SP100 Feb240 ..	15888	15089	4⅛	2	3½ −	¾	235.18
SP100 Feb240 p	2085	3224	11⅝	7⅞	8⅛ +	¼	235.18
SP100 Feb245 ..	17784	14235	2 3-16	1	1 15-16 −	7-16	235.18
SP100 Feb245 p	494	2717	15	11½	12½ +	1	235.18
SP100 Feb250 ..	9904	13319	1 1-16	½	13-16 −	⅜	235.18
SP100 Feb250 p	50	65	19¼	16½	19¼ +	4	235.18
SP100 Feb255 ..	5306	10900	½	3-16	⅜ −	3-16	235.18
SP100 Mar210 p	955	2666	¾	7-16	7-16 −	1-16	235.18
SP100 Mar215 ..	149	120	21¾	19⅞	2... −	¾	235.18
SP100 Mar215 p	9321	4237	1⅜	11-16	... −	1-16	235.18
SP100 Mar220 ..	118	2874	17⅛	13½	17⅛ −	1	235.18
SP100 Mar220 p	5547	7230	2⅜	1 5-16	1½	......	235.18
SP100 Mar225 ..	60	1300	14	10¾	14		235.18
SP100 Mar225 p	1608	3028	4¼	2 9-16	2 9-16 −	⅛	235.18
SP100 Mar230 ..	256	693	10	7	9½ −	2	235.18
SP100 Mar230 p	2288	3090	6¼	4	4⅞	......	235.18
SP100 Mar235 ..	9..	...	7½		7...		235.18
S~~...~~	737	2890		6¼	6½	......	235.18
SP100 Mar240 ..	1361	2213	5½	3¼	4¾ −	⅞	235.18
SP100 Mar240 p	333	458	12¾	9	9½ +	⅝	235.18

The excerpted chart of the Dow Jones Industrials on a previous page tells us that January 1987 saw a strong market. Consequently, we never did have a chance to make any further purchases in the February 255 Call Options. But we *did* have *30* Options at this juncture, which had cost us a total of *$1,062.*

As the early-1987 market coasted into February, the strength did not equal that of January, but new highs *were* made. In the final week for the Options — expiration day was Friday, February 20th — as seen on the Option table to the right (courtesy of **Barron's**), the February 255 Call Option (arrow) hit a high of *23.*

The Option *had* to sell at 23, because the Index at that time touched *278.* (The Index Price of 278 minus the Striking Price of 255 equals 23.)

What are 30 Options worth at 23? Well, one Option is worth $2,300, 10 Options are worth $23,000, and *30* Options are worth 30 x 2300, or *$69,000.*

The February 255 Call Options had seen a *$1,062* investment become worth *$69,000* in 7 weeks.

February 23, 1987

BARRON'S

Chicago Board

S&P 100 INDEX

Expire date Strike price	Open Sales	Int.	Week's's High	Low	Price	Net Chg.	Close
SP100 Feb220..	65	81	55½	54½	54½+	6½	275.06
SP100 Feb225..	153	322	51½	45½	49½+	8½	275.06
SP100 Feb225 p	355	47734	1-16	1-16	1-16	......	275.06
SP100 Feb230..	198	856	46¾	43	43 +	3¼	275.06
SP100 Feb230 p	1040	58219	1-16	1-16	1-16	......	275.06
SP100 Feb235..	1416	3186	42	36	37½+	3½	275.06
SP100 Feb235 p	1045	64342	1-16	1-16	1-16	......	275.06
SP100 Feb240..	3516	6653	37½	30½	34⅜+	4⅞	275.06
SP100 Feb240 p	1084	81881	1-16	1-16	1-16	......	275.06
SP100 Feb245..	5826	12970	33	26	30⅛+	6	275.06
SP100 Feb245 p	1384	89180	1-16	1-16	1-16	......	275.06
SP100 Feb250..	7804	16222	28	20⅞	25⅛+	5⅝	275.06
SP100 Feb250 p	4991	79148	1-16	1-16	1-16	...:...	275.06
SP100 Feb255..	14339	21598	23	15½	20 +	5¼	275.06
SP100 Feb255 p	18922	70741	⟍	1-16	1-16-	⅛	275.06
SP100 Feb260..	24482	17092	18	10¾	15 +	5⅛	275.06
SP100 Feb260 p	34183	75398	5-1¢	1-16	1-16-5-16		275.06
SP100 Feb265..	68895	24449	13	6¼	10⅛+	4½	275.06
SP100 Feb265 p	61313	49510	1 1-16	1-16	1-16-	1⅛	275.06
SP100 Feb270	235408	43614	8¾	2⅝	5 +2 11-16		275.06
SP100 Feb270 p	144934	49322	2½	1-16	1-16-3 1-16		275.06
SP100 Feb275..	310171	57038	3½	1-16	1-16-	⅝	275.06
SP100 Feb275 p	108692	27998	5⅝	1-16	1-16-6 13-16		275.06
SP100 Feb280	107170	45102		1-16	1-16		275.06
SP100 Feb285..		2063	¼	1-16	1-16	......	275.06
SP100 Feb285 p	747	510	14	8	12 -	5½	275.06

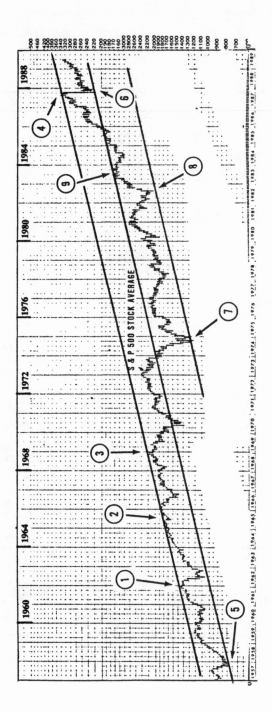

S & P 500 STOCK AVERAGE

THIS IS THE MOST IMPORTANT STOCK MARKET CHART YOU WILL EVER SEE!

Because of its importance, which will soon be self-demonstrable, we turn these pages around so that text will face the chart, and we also reproduce the chart on each succeeding page so that there will be no "page turning" to follow the ideas as they are set forth.

This chart enabled us to "call" the October 1987 market crash *well* before the event, and this same chart is *again* flying the red flag of danger for current markets, as we write. Getting the timing right on the 1987 market debacle was the immediate cause of the $2,000 to $192,400 result with the October 285 Put Index Options. The opportunities now shaping up with Index Options may not necessarily eventuate on the same scale as was true for us in 1987, but will still be

of remarkable profit potential, as we see it.

This time around, economic *recession* will probably coincide with another devastating market slide, which will create historic opportunities among the hundreds of long-term *Warrants* trading today. And the same is true for hundreds of *Convertibles* which will land on the bargain counter, as 10 and 20-year "Calls" on promising common stocks, where potential capital appreciation in a subsequent market recovery, and high yields, will make them *particularly* attractive for tax-advantaged retirement plans.

ALL the above being true, we ask the reader to pay full attention to following the concepts we shall now describe.

Any Trend Line is formed by two tops or two bottoms in stock market movement. When they are connected, they *very often* provide highly

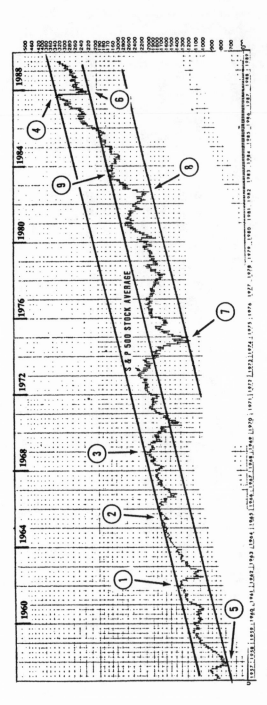

S & P 500 STOCK AVERAGE

82

never again was touched by market action until the October 1987 market top at (4).

We trust that the reader is sufficiently impressed by the fact that a Trend Line which was recognizeable in 1962, 1966 and 1968 could perfectly catch a *momentous* market top in *1987*, nineteen years later!

This sharply emphasizes the truth of the fact that the same *cycles* which are present in *all* living things, and in the physical world around us as well (the seasonal migration of birds and the tides, to name but two cycles) are everywhere in the stock market. You just have to be aware of them.

Continuing with the development of the chart, a *lower* Trend Line, drawn through the 1957 bottom at (5), *parallel* to the upper Trend Line, did not call many turns *until* the important *1983 top* (9) hit the Trend Line, and, *most*

useful guidance to the stock market movement which follows. As a Trend Line continues on its path, other short-term and long-term Trend Lines fall into place, such action corroborating the forecasting value of the original Trend Line.

In this case, we drew the original Trend Line, joining (1) and (2), the 1962 and 1966 market tops respectively, *about 23 years ago*, and have followed it since on a very regular basis, the chart appearing in the issues of the **R.H.M Survey** on many occasions.

Let us immediately set forth the *most remarkable* projection for this Trend Line, which meant a great deal to the subscribers to the Survey in 1987, safeguarding, and enhancing, their capital, as we shall soon document.

The original Trend Line was reinforced at (3), the important *late-1968* top, presaging the steep 1969-1970 market slide. This Trend Line, then,

S & P 500 STOCK AVERAGE

84

remarkable, the *late-1987 bottom* at (6).

A third (lowest) Trend Line, drawn parallel to the other two Trend Lines, through the pivotal *1974 bottom,* had the following meaning: A Trend Channel composed of the middle Trend Line and the lowest Trend Line, encompassed all market action from late-*1974* through *1985,* when, for the first time, the market broke through the middle Trend Line on the upside, setting forth the huge market rally of 1986-1987, and setting the stage for the October 1987 debacle.

Another way of understanding this 32-year chart, is to realize that there are only two Trend Channels involved. The upper Trend Channel encompassed all market activity from 1957 through 1973, with only one mild aberration: the 1970 bear market developed such momentum that it broke through the lower Trend Line for a

few months, but then quickly re-entered the Channel, because *it wasn't time yet* to decisively break that Trend Line.

The *right* time came in late-1973 when the lower Trend Line of the original Channel was smashed on the downside.

For the time being, the upper Trend Channel went out of business, giving way to the lower Trend Channel, to which we have already had reference. When the market broke through the upper Trend Line of this lower Trend Channel in 1985, market action *re-entered the original Trend Channel,* and has remained in that Channel to this date.

Note all through the 32 years of the chart, how many times market action hit a Trend Line and *bounced away* from that Trend Line with varying amounts of force, providing important guidance for many stock market approaches.

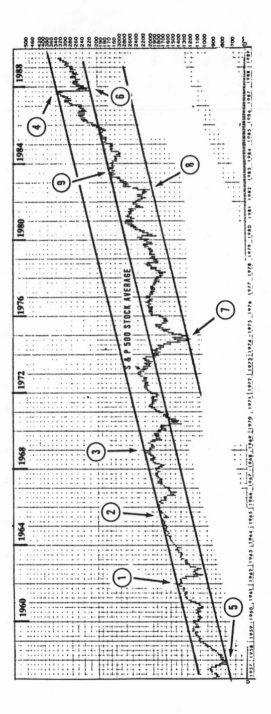

S & P 500 STOCK AVERAGE

86

It was in this light that we regarded the approach of the 1987 market towards the upper Trend Line. But this would be no *ordinary* "bounce," because of the runaway power of the 1987 market, the increasing intensity of "Futures-Related Program Trading," which, as we have already described, *accelerates* market movement, and, also, the great *instabilities* and *lack of soundness*, which had been built into the stock and bond markets and the economy, on *a worldwide basis.*

In 1987, we began sounding the alarm in the pages of the **R.H.M. Survey**, as follows:

In the **R.H.M. Survey** of August 28, 1987, which happened to also be the issue where we first recommended purchase of the *October 285 Put Index Options*, we stated:

"The *stock market rise* has also lasted five years (along with the expansion of the economy) . . . And it has been a *prodigious* advance in the United States, joined in by runaway upside markets in many parts of the world — Tokyo, London, Hong Kong, and even in totally unlikely places such as Mexico City and Manila, and other secondary financial centers where near-bankruptcy is the universal condition . . . ''

And then we added the following:

"Every yardstick of value, every historical perspective, emphasizes the inevitable judgment that we are near a turning point to the downside . . . '' (Original emphasis.)

In the Survey of September 11, 1987, we stated:

" . . . The elements that *created* the market rise since 1974, capped by the upside explosion of 1986-1987, ensure that *something big is going to happen on the downside.* This still leaves a question mark hanging over the simple word — when? — and to our way of thinking, the answer has to be: not so far in the future that you should not be preparing for it *now.*" (Original emphasis.)

Meanwhile, in our **R.H.M. Convertible Survey** of October 2, 1987, two weeks before the crash, we stated:

"We have no doubt that a full-fledged bear market is in the offing . . . In adequately preparing for these prospects, the *first* imperative must be to establish *liquidity.* If a very large part of your funds is in stocks and bonds, your losses could be extremely painful in quick order, since a bear market typically strikes with great speed, and does not allow much time to pare holdings. *That* has to be done while the financial skies are still relatively blue . . . " (Original emphasis.)

Remaining constantly aware of the approach of the 1987 market towards that all-important, 30-year Trend Line (1957 - 1987), we made our first "Buy" recommendation for the October 285 Put Index Option in the Survey of August 28, 1987.

This was the issue where we had stated that "Every yardstick of value, every historical perspective, emphasizes the inevitable judgment that we are near a turning point to the downside . . . "

Friday, September 4, 1987

Chicago Board

S&P 100 INDEX

Strike Price	Calls–Last Sep	Oct	Nov	Puts–Last Sep	Oct	Nov
280	39	....	....	1/16	....	....
285	30	....	33⅝	⅛	¾	1 11/16
290	23½	29½	....	¼	1⅜	2½
295	21	22¼	26	9/16	2	3⅞
300	14	18¾	22½	1	3⅛	5
305	10	14½	19	2 1/16	4⅝	6¼
310	6⅜	11½	15¾	3⅞	7	8⅝
315	3¾	8½	12	6⅛	9⅜	10
320	2 1/16	6⅜	10	9½	12	14½
325	1 3/16	4⅜	7⅞	13½	15½	17
330	⅝	3¼	6¼	18⅜	20	20
335	5/16	2 3/16	4¾	22½	21½	24¼
340	⅛	1 7/16	3½	26½	27	28
345	1/16	15/16	2⅞	29½	32	32½
350	1/16	11/16	1¾	....	....	....

Total call volume 184,846 Total call open int. 673,216
Total put volume 187,038 Total put open int. 762,856
The index: High 318.74; Low 312.76; Close 312.92, −3.95

We began by stating: " . . . Labor Day falls on Monday, September 7th this year, which is one week from the time subscribers get this issue of the Survey. *We would own* Put Index Options in the week to come . . . we would buy the October *285* Put Index Option at whatever price it is selling, but not above the 5/8 level. And we would make this purchase on Friday, September 4th, directly preceding Labor Day." (Original emphasis.) The Index Option table for the close of Fri-

Thursday, September 10, 1987

Chicago Board

S&P 100 INDEX

Strike Price	Calls–Last			Puts–Last		
	Sep	Oct	Nov	Sep	Oct	Nov
260	54	....	....	....	....	....
270	43	....	....	....	....	....
280	33¼	...	....	1/16	....	....
285	28¾	29	31¼	1/16	⅝	1⅝
290	23	26	27¾	1/16	1	2½
295	18¾	21¼	....	3/16	1⅝	3⅜
300	14	17½	20¼	7/16	2 11/16	5⅛
305	9½	13¾	17½	1	4	6½
310	5⅝	10⅞	14¼	2 5/16	5⅞	8¼
315	2 15/16	8⅛	11⅜	4⅝	8⅛	11¼
320	1¼	5¾	9¼	8⅛	11⅜	13
325	7/16	4	7½	12⅜	14¼	17½
330	3/16	2 11/16	5⅝	17¼	18¼	20⅜
335	1/16	1¾	4½	22¼	23¼	23
340	1/16	1⅛	3⅜	27	28	28
345	1/16	¾	2½	32½	33	....
350	1/16	7/16	1 13/16	37¼	....	....

Total call volume 228,422 Total call open int. 855,882
Total put volume 173,243 Total put open int. 742,684
The index: High 313.54; Low 310.36; Close 312.85, +2.79.

day, September 4th (courtesy of the **Wall Street Journal**) shows the October 285 Put Options closing at *3/4*, but the Option also sold freely at *5/8 during* the day, so the purchase was made, with the next purchase to be at *1/4* in line with the Dollar Averaging approach which always accompanies such purchases, and which we explained on a previous page.

That is, whether the first purchase is at 1/2, 9/16 or at 5/8, the *next* purchase is at 1/4, to get back in line with our standard scale down purchases of equal dollar amounts at 1/4, 1/8 and 1/16, *if* the Option gets that low.

And for those subscribers who had gone away for a long Labor Day weekend without entering an open order, September 10th provided another opportunity at 5/8, as shown in the table for that date on the preceding page, and the following day, the October 285 Put Option closed at *7/16*.

The next stop in Dollar Averaging was at *1/4*, and this was accomplished in the week ending September 25th, *along with* the next purchase at *1/8*, the weekly Index Option summary in **Barron's** for 9-28-87 (see next page) showing the Option selling as low as 1/8 (arrow).

Finally, the week ending October 2nd, as shown in **Barron's** for 10-5-87 (see page 93), saw The October 285 Put Option sell down to the *1/16* level, and the Dollar Averaging package was complete.

Working with $500 Units,

8 Options had been purchased at 5/8 for $500

20 Options had been purchased at 1/4 for $500

40 Options had been purchased at 1/8 for $500

80 Options had been purchased at 1/16 for $500

A total of *148* Options had been purchased for *$2,000.*

September 28, 1987

BARRON'S

Chicago Board

S&P 100 INDEX

Expire date Strike price	Open Sales	Week's Int	High	Low	Net Price	Chg.	N.Y. Close
SP100 Oct285..	137	1110	32½	22¾	30¾+	2¾	314.88
SP100 Oct285 p.	21378	30255	⅞	⅛	3-16−	3-16	314.88
SP100 Oct290..	461	2215	28	16½	25¼+	3	314.88
SP100 Oct290 p.	40597	34237	1 9-16	¼	¼−	7-16	314.88
SP100 Oct295..	943	2423	23¾	12½	21 +	3½	314.88
SP100 Oct295 p	50766	37709	2 11-16	½	9-16−	¾	314.88
SP100 Oct300..	6685	6952	20¼	9⅛	16½+	2¾	314.88
SP100 Oct300 p	110031	54350	4½	1	1 16−1	5-16	314.88
SP100 Oct305..	30308	12679	16	6⅛	13 +	3	314.88
SP100 Oct305 p	111807	58744	6⅝	1¾	1 13-16−2	1-16	314.88
SP100 Oct310..	72247	32902	11⅛	3¾	9⅞+	2⅞	314.88
SP100 Oct310 p	108200	51981	9½	3	3⅛−	3	314.88
SP100 Oct315..	156403	44614	8¾	2½	6¾+	1⅞	314.88
SP100 Oct315 p	65661	33685	13¼	4⅞	4⅞−	4⅛	314.88
SP100 Oct320..	144540	55344	6⅛	1½	4⅜+	1¼	314.88
SP100 Oct320 p	25465	17464	17	7½	8⅛−	4¼	314.88
SP100 Oct325..	109566	47374	4⅛	13-16	2⅝+	11-16	314.88
SP100 Oct325 p	5361	6425	22	10½	11¾−	4¾	314.88
SP100 Oct330...	93433	53419	2⅝	7-16	1 7-16+	5-16	314.88
SP100 Oct330 p	1525	2584	26½	13¾	15⅝−	5⅞	314.88
SP100 Oct335..	58706	43506	1 7-16	¼	11-16+	⅛	314.88
SP100 Oct335 p	96	192	31	18¼	20½−	5¾	314.88
SP100 Oct340..	35017	37779	⅞	⅛	5-16.....		314.88
SP100 Oct340 p	101	79	32	24	27 −	1¾	314.88
SP100 Oct345...	22715	29364	½	1-16	3-16+	1-16	314.88
SP100 Oct350..	22855	32348	5-16	1-16	⅛......		314.88
SP100 Nov285..	258	3376	34½	28½	32 +	4¾	314.88
SP100 Nov285 p	9495	15714	2¼	13-16	15-16−	3-16	314.88
SP100 Nov290..	216	223	30¼	22½	29⅜+	5⅜	314.88
SP100 Nov290 p	7879	11085	3⅝	1⅜	1 9-16−	½	314.88

October 5, 1987

BARRON'S

Chicago Board

S&P 100 INDEX

Expire date Strike price		Sales	Open Int.	Week's High	Low	Price	Net Chg.	N.Y. Close
SP100	Oct285..	96	1107	36	31	36	+ 5¼	321.64
SP100	Oct285 p	22432	43537	⅛	1-16	1-16—	⅛	321.64
SP100	Oct290..	134	2205	32	26	31⅞+	6⅝	321.64
SP100	Oct290 p.	26979	36817	¼	1-16	1-16—3-16		321.64
SP100	Oct295..	197	2375	27¾	21	7½+	6½	321.64
SP100	Oct295 p.	37253	39800	½	1-16	⅛—7-16		321.64
SP100	Oct300..	1457	6486	23¼	16	22¼+	5¾	321.64
SP100	Oct300 p	69205	60160	1	3-16	¼—13-16		321.64
SP100	Oct305..	6130	11593	18½	11⅜	17⅝+	4⅝	321.64
SP100	Oct305 p	107084	68715	2	⅜	⅜—1 7-16		321.64
SP100	Oct310..	34140	34012	14⅜	8⅛	13¼+	3⅜	321.64
SP100	Oct310 p	127578	62463	3½	13-16	15-16—2 3-16		321.64
SP100	Oct315..	131189	46116	10¼	5⅛	9⅛+	2⅜	321.64
SP100	Oct315 p	135052	38164	5⅝	1 11-16	1 15-16—2 15-16		321.64
SP100	Oct320..	186719	62617	6⅝	3⅛	5⅞+	1½	321.64
SP100	Oct320 p	65092	21224	8⅝	3¼	3¾—	4⅜	321.64
SP100	Oct325..	161152	55084	4	1⅝	3¼+	⅝	321.64
SP100	Oct325 p	13645	6801	12	5⅝	6⅜—	5⅜	321.64
SP100	Oct330...	148096	66011	2¼	13-16	1⅝+3-16		321.64
SP100	Oct330 p	2711	2234	16½	9	9⅝—	6	321.64
SP100	Oct335..	61055	47553	1 3-16	⅜	11-16......		321.64
SP100	Oct335 p	589	129	20⅛	14	14 —	6½	321.64
SP100	Oct340...	26410	41767	⅝	⅛	¼—1-16		321.64
SP100	Oct345..	10568	30829	5-16	1-16	1-16—	⅛	321.64
SP100	Oct345 p	122	1	30¾	24½	24½—14		321.64
SP100	Oct350...	10581	40796	3-16	1-16	1-16—1-16		321.64

The reason we were able to carry through the entire Dollar Averaging program in this instance is to be found in the chart of the Dow Jones Industrials as it appeared in **Barron's** for October 5, 1987, shown on the following page.

Making a saw-tooth pattern to the downside after Labor Day, a subsequent market rally moved up to 2660 for the Industrials two weeks before the market crash, pushing Put Index Options *to the downside*.

On Friday, October 16, 1989, one day before the October 19th 600-point crash in the Dow Jones Industrials, the stock market plunged with only about 1/6th the intensity of the Monday crash, but it was enough to whirl the October 285 Put Options to a remarkable profit.

We will interject at this point that we always *welcome* a contrary market movement following the first purchase in a Dollar Averaging program. Thus, if we buy *Call* Options and the market goes into retreat, rather than bewail the market going "the other way," we welcome the opportunity to make further purchases at lower prices.

For with each purchase, the average price of the Options purchased goes down sharply, *and* we have many more Options with which to benefit from a "reversal." And considerable movement in *one* direction in the stock market *often* leads to a reversal, whereupon the profits from a completed Dollar Averaging program is always, automatically, *very large*. Of course, the week ending October 16 was in a class by itself! The headline (see page 96) from the Saturday, October 17, 1987 **New**

October 5, 1987

B A R R O N ' S

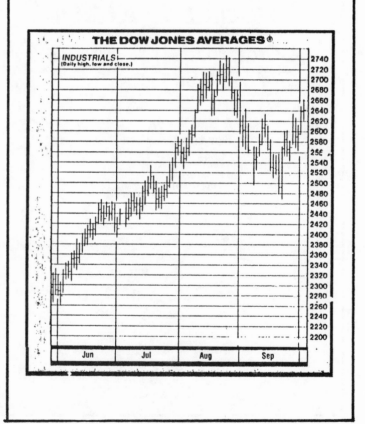

THE DOW JONES AVERAGES®

INDUSTRIALS
(Daily high, low and close.)

SATURDAY, OCTOBER 17, 1987

STOCK PRICES FALL ON A BROAD FRONT; VOLUME IS RECORD

A Crossroad For Wall St.

DOW DROPS 108.36

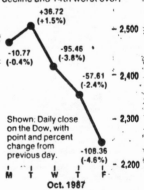

A Bad Week For the Dow

Falling 235.48 points, or 9.49 percent, from Monday's opening of 2,482.21, this was the worst postwar week of decline and 14th worst ever.

+36.72
(+1.5%)

− 2,500

-10.77
(-0.4%)

-95.46
(-3.8%)

-57.61
(-2.4%)

− 2,400

Shown: Daily close on the Dow, with point and percent change from previous day.

− 2,300

-108.36
(-4.6%)

− 2,200

M T W T F

Oct. 1987

The New York Times/Oct. 17, 1987

York Times, plus the accompanying chart tells it all.

Friday, October 16, 1987

Chicago Board

S&P 100 INDEX

Strike Price	Calls—Last			Puts—Last		
	Oct	Nov	Dec	Oct	Nov	Dec
280	....	8⅞	12	....	13¾	16⅞
285	1/16	6¾	11	10	17	18½
290	1/16	5⅜	9½	15	21	22
295	1/16	4¼	9	21	24	25
300	1/16	3¼	6¾	26	29	29
305	1/16	2½	5½	31	33½	32½
310	1/16	1 13/16	4½	36	37	37¼
315	1/16	1 5/16	3¾	40½	42½	41
320	1/16	⅞	3	45	48	44
325	1/16	9/16	2⅛	53½	50	47
330	1/16	7/16	1⅝	48	62½	49
335	1/16	5/16	1 7/16	47	53	....
340	1/16	¼	1 1/16	....	....	....
345	1/16	⅛	¾	59	59¾	....
350	....	1/16	½	....	....	....

Total call volume 435,888   Total call open int. 1,086,854
Total put volume 494,931   Total put open int. 530,490
The index: High 291.49; Low 273.52; Close 274.13, −15.95

Finally, we present the Index Option table for the close on October 16th (courtesy of the **Wall Street Journal**) showing the October 285 Put Options closing the day at *10.*

But the weekly record from **Barron's** for October 19th, giving the close for week ending October 16th, shows an actual intra-day high of *13.*

Since our Dollar Averaging program had ended up with *148* October 285 Put Options, which had cost a total of *$2,000*, a high at 13 meant the following:

1 Option at 13 has a value of $ 1,300

10 Options at 13 have a value of $ 13,000

100 Options at 13 have a value of $ 130,000

and 148 Options at 13 have a value of $ 192,400

An investment in the October 285 Put Index Options had seen *$2,000* become worth *$192,400* in six weeks time.

The November 285 Put Index Options

With the full complement of *October* 285 Put Index Options having been purchased, utilizing Dollar Averaging, we did not forget the *November* 285 Put Index Options. In the October 9, 1987 issue of the **R.H.M. Survey**, we advised as follows:

" . . . the *November 285 Put Options* for the S & P 100 Index should be purchased if a rallying market brings them down to the 1/2 level, with a 'Dollar Averaging' approach then utilized."

Following the writing of those words, the market did just that — have something of a rally — and the November 285 Put Index Options sold down to 3/8,

Monday, October 19, 1987

Chicago Board

S&P 100 INDEX

Strike Price	Calls–Last			Puts–Last		
	Nov	Dec	Jan	Nov	Dec	Jan
255	8¼	12	20	70	70	18
260	7	12½	21	76	75	23
265	5¾	7	15	80	87	115
270	5	8	12	83	95	110
275	4	8	15	88	99	55
280	3¾	8	10½	93	100	55
285	2¾	6½	8¾	100	100	91
290	2⅛	5¾	9½	103	105	105
295	1½	5	7½	108	115	84
300	1½	3⅞	7	111	115	60
305	1	3	6¼	118	130	90
310	⅞	2¾	5	123	145	135
315	11/16	1¾	4¼	125	150	140
320	½	1⅝	4	129	150	87
325	5/16	1 7/16	3⅛	135	70	137
330	¼	1⅛	2¾	150	150	....
335	⅛	¾	2½	142	165	104
340	⅛	⅝	2	150	....	....
345	1/16	¾	....	155	89	....
350	1/16	7/16	....	155	100	....

Total call volume 177,590 Total call open int. 1,305,927
Total put volume 145,701 Total put open int. 257,321
The index: High 274.13; Low 216.31; Close 216.31, −57.82

making possible the first purchase at 1/2, or 10 Options at 1/2 for $500, using that same "unit" of purchase. The November 285 Put Option did not get below the 3/8 level, so a purchase at 1/4 was never possible. But even the one purchased performed spectacularly on Monday, October 19th, when the S & P 100 Index fell *57.82 points*. As can be seen on the Index Option table for October 19, 1987 (courtesy of the **Wall Street Journal**), although worth only 68.69 on immediate exercise value (285 minus 216.31) a large *premium* was being paid for this Option by speculators who were looking for the Index to go down another few hundred points. So (see arrow) the November 285 Put Index Options closed on Monday's market at *100!*

One Index Option selling at 100 has a market value of *$10,000*, and since the position had *10* Options, they were worth $100,000.

An investment in 10 November 285 Put Index Options at 1/2 had seen a *$500* investment become worth *$100,000* in less than two weeks time.

Pyramiding With Index Options

Now we leave the superheated atmosphere of the October 1987 market crash, and remind the reader that there are plenty of "fireworks" with Index Options *without* a market crash. Remember that with the *February 255 Call Options*, an investment of $1,062 had become worth $69,000 in early-1987.

For capital building with Index Options, we *highly* recommend *Pyramiding*, which can be used in conjunction with Dollar Averaging, and which basically is a process where you increase the size of your commitment, using profits from a previous success.

In its barest form — something we do not necessarily recommend, as we shall soon discuss, but is descriptive of the process — it would work as follows:

You invest $625 in 100 Index Options at 1/16, and a run in the market causes that Option to go to *1*. At 1, your 100 Options are worth *$10,000*. A move from 1/16 to 1 is hardly unknown in the Index Options market, and can happen without the Index price actually reaching the Strike price of the Option. All it requires is for speculators to get excited about a market move — usually involving a "reversal," which action is the best friend of an Index Option!

To give some idea of that action, consider that the market is having some good-sized *declines*, so that *Call* Index Options are doing what they normally do in such circumstances — drop precipitously. A Call Option, with the market going the other way (down) is also, say, 25 points out of the money, so it is selling at a lowly 1/16. The market hits a certain point — say a *Trend Line*, as in our previous discussion — and *reverses course*, bouncing vigorously to the upside.

Depending on the size of the "bounce," or perhaps two or three days of back-to-back advances, the Index Option position is now only *15* points out of the money, and speculators are getting excited about the rise in the market. In such circumstances, the Index Option can easily hit that $1 mark, from its 1/16 beginning.

So our first sequence has seen a $500 investment become worth $10,000 in a 1/16 to 1 move. Now, the speculator waits for another 1/16 opportunity to develop, and either one will do — a Put or a Call. Let us say that now a *Put* Index Option is getting cheaper and cheaper as the market *advances*, and one Put Option sells at 1/16 because it is, again, 25 points out of the money and the market looks "hot" on the upside.

Here is where the Pyramiding comes into the picture. Our speculator is "going for broke" — looking for a very large profit on an initially small investment. Liking the outlook for that Put Option at 1/16 — expecting the advancing market to shift to *falling* — he takes his previous $10,000 profit and uses $6,250 of it to purchase 1,000 Options at 1/16, at a cost of $6,250. This means he still has $3,750 remaining of his original profit.

Again there is a market reversal, and the Put Index Option reaches 1. At 1, 1,000 Options are worth

102

$100,000. So the original $625 investment has become worth *$103,750.*

We pause here for a rather strange set of events in late-1985 — strange, but very enlightening! — when we were explaining Pyramiding to subscribers to the **R.H.M. Survey,** and were pointing to the November 265 Call Options for the *Major Market Index* (which trades on the American Stock Exchange, and basically parallels the movement of the Dow Jones Industrial Average). The November 265 Calls were selling at 3/16, and we were discussing purchasing *50* Options at a cost of *$937.*

Up ran those Options to sell at *7/8,* where the 50 Options were worth *$4,375.* At this point, explaining Pyramiding, we pointed now to the *December* 275 Call Option, selling at the same 3/16 for the new Option as where we had started in the first place, and we stated that if one took the entire $4,375 that had accrued with the first success, it would now buy *233* December 275 Call Index Options at its then price of 3/16.

We do not know whether any subscriber actually did this, because this was all by way of *explanation* of Pyramiding, but the market continued to move higher, and 5 weeks later, the December 275 Call Options were selling at *6-5/8,* where 233 Options were worth *$154,362.*

The story continues. The market moved still higher, with short-sellers panicking and money managers going in for frantic buying with their multi-billion dollar pension funds, so that the Major Market Index reached *296*. Now, at 296, a *275* Call is worth 296 minus 275, or *21*, and that is where the December 275 Call Option sold.

1 Option at 21 is worth $ 2,100

10 Options at 21 are worth $ 21,000

100 Options at 21 are worth $ 210,000

and 233 Options at 21 are worth $ 495,125

$ 937 had become worth *$ 495,125* in a *very* successful two-step *Pyramiding*.

As it happened, we were using all the above actual market prices for Options for the Major Market Index to *explain* Pyramiding in the pages of the **R.H.M Survey,** and we have no idea whether any subscriber did some or all of the "Pyramiding."

But the *important* thing to note is how such a large profit could develop from a small investment *without* a headline-making stock market crash. We feel strongly that Dollar Averaging and Pyramiding with low-price Index Options *are* capable of producing remarkable profits by following the proper guidelines.

So Pyramiding works by taking profits from one success to make a *larger* commitment, to aim at a *second* success, and it is an attractive process, because even in an "all-out" Pyramiding, you are using only a tiny bit of original capital, and the proceeds of the first success for all the rest. In Las Vegas or Atlantic City terms, you are "playing with the house's money."

Anyone who wishes to do so, can, of course, go for an all-out Pyramiding, with the high nervous strain that this implies, but we favor a more moderate approach. Thus, if we go back to our first success of $625 to $10,000 in a 1/16 to 1 move, and another opportunity with an Option at 1/16 comes into view, suppose we purchased *500* Options at 1/16 for $3,125?

We would still have $6,875 of the profits from our first success remaining, and if the Option then proceeded to run up to, say, the *2* level, the 500 Options would still be worth $100,000.

Or, for the second run, one could take even a *smaller* portion of that first profit, and since the leverage potential of a very low-price Index Option is *so* great, a noticeable move in the market could *still* produce a very large profit.

And at a point where one had *two* successes to one's credit, one could then take on some greater risks with what is by now a nicely expanding capital base, increasing the size of commitments still further.

Pyramiding with low-price Index Options can be a very *important* means of building capital.

Interim Conclusion

Later in the book there are some additional discussions about different levels of "Opportunities with Index Options," but at this point we want to emphasize the *basic*, and *logical* underpinning of this entire concept.

When we make speculative commitments with an Index Option, we typically make *small* investments. But when an Index Option speculation enjoys a success, it, again typically, produces a very *large* profit. The extent of such profits can run to tens of thousands of dollars, from Index Option investments of $500 or $1,000.

Consequently, one can have one, two, three, even four or five losses in a row, and when one success is scored, it typically wipes away all the previous losses and ends up with a *very* large net profit. If one, then, *keeps* individual commitments small (small in relation to one's total funds that are available for speculative building of capital), we feel that substantial profits are probable.

We have described many Index Option successes which produced *very* large profits. Obviously, there were also numbers of *losses* interspersed with the successes, but our experience has most distinctly been that totaling up the losses produces a figure which is *insignificant* when compared with the profits. *That* is the logical basis of Index Option speculation, and we feel that it remains very true that low-price, high-leverage Index Options are one of the best means of building capital in the stock market.

CURRENT SUPPLEMENT AVAILABLE

As this book was going to press, important developments were taking place. Long-Term *Warrants* on dozens of the most important Japanese companies, already trading in Europe, will, before too long, trade in the United States as well.

Stock Index *Futures* and Stock Index *Options* on the Japanese stock markets are already trading in Japan and elsewhere, and are preparing to trade in the United States. They will be highly-important speculative mediums, along the lines set forth in this book.

In the **Current Supplement,** the latest approaches to Index Option speculation are described, in light of the most recent stock market action.

In addition, the Current Supplement contains a valuable alphabetical listing by *Industry Group*, of all Warrants, Convertibles and Scores trading today, plus other current information important in today's market, regarding these fields.

The publishers of this book would like to send you this Current Supplement. Just send your name and address to:

Current Supplement, Department 96
R.H.M. Press
172 Forest Avenue
Glen Cove, New York 11542

There is no cost or obligation.

WARRANTS

Where **Index Options** are the most highly-leveraged *short-term* speculative instrument in the stock market, **Warrants** are the most highly-leveraged *long-term* speculative instrument. Just as with Index Options, Warrants are very amenable to mathematical logic, and with a good understanding of what Warrants are, and how they operate, very substantial stock market profits can result. While Index Options earn their profits by reacting to the movement of the *stock market as a whole*, the fortunes of each Warrant is inextricably tied to the movement of *its common stock*.

A Warrant is issued by the corporation itself and represents the right to buy a share of common stock of the company at a specific price, for a specific period of time. This "time" period is always measured in *years*, 3 years, 5 years, at times even 10 years, in contrast with *Index Options* which have a life measured in *months*. When a company gets *into* trouble, the common stock can decline sharply, but the *Warrant,* can fall to a very low figure — even pennies. Then, when the company gets *out* of trouble, the common stock will recover, but the *Warrant* can soar in percentage terms. Thus in later pages we describe how with **GEICO** Warrants, *$500* became worth *$608,000* in just such a "swing" in fortunes for that company. The most important characteristic of a Warrant is its *leverage*, its ability to appreciate at a far greater rate than its respective common stock, and we shall begin by recounting how a $500 investment in **R.K.O. Warrants**, quite remarkably became worth $104,000, as the common stock first nosedived, and then recovered.

At this point, however, let us consider the crucial difference in behavior between a Warrant that is selling "in the money" — that is, having intrinsic value because the common stock price is *above* the exercise price of the Warrant — and a Warrant that is selling "out of the money," — the common stock price being *below* the exercise price of the Warrant.

Let us consider an XYZ Warrant that is the right to buy XYZ common stock at $10 per share, and also consider that XYZ common is selling at 15. The XYZ Warrant *must* sell at least at 5 in this instance, because if the Warrant were to sell significantly *below* 5, "arbitrageurs" would step in to make a riskless profit.

To explain this, suppose the XYZ Warrants were selling at *3* when the common is at 15, even though each Warrant can be turned in to the corporation with $10, to receive one share of common stock. An arbitrageur could buy one Warrant for $3, turn the Warrant in to the company with $10 payment, for a total outlay of $13, and then turn around and sell the share of stock he duly received, for *$15*. His profit would be $2, and there would have been no risk in the transaction.

Indeed, the arbitrageur would not wait to receive his share of stock from the company before selling it in the open market, because during the time he was waiting to get that share, the market price of the stock could go through some changes. Instead, as soon as he had purchased his Warrant at 3, he would have *sold one share of XYZ common short* at 15, thereby locking in his profit. In later pages, we will be explaining the very important practice of "short-selling," since a great many investors have little understanding of it, or, at best, have a distorted picture of what it encompasses. And a knowledge of what short-selling entails will play a part in understanding various approaches to each of the major areas covered in this book.

Having established that with XYZ common selling at 15, the XYZ Warrant, exerciseable at 10, *must* sell *at least* at 5, it is further true that the Warrant can sell *above* its straight exercise value, to reflect the additional exercise life still remaining. So a Warrant can sell *above* its straight exercise value — at a premium —, but cannot sell *below* its straight exercise value — at a discount.

What is the case, however, when the common stock is selling *below* the exercise price of the Warrant? Here, the XYZ Warrant is still the right to buy XYZ common stock at 10, but the current market price of that XYZ common is, say, 7. No one would exercise a Warrant at an expenditure price of $10, if he can buy that same share of common stock in the open market for $7, *without* a Warrant. Here, there is no objective criterion for fixing a minimum price for an out of the money Warrant. It can sell down as far as it wants to as far as the arbitrageur is concerned — it has no minimum value.

Because this is so, emotion can have full sway with an out of the money Warrant, erring on the side of pessimism, or on the side of optimism. If the general market is on a steady course, or is heading higher, the Warrant may be generously priced, but if the company that issued the Warrant is doing poorly — or is even in serious trouble — and the general market is on the *downside*, the Warrant can sell down to a *very* low price, getting down to a few dollars, or one dollar, or even the "pennies" level, because investors have little faith that the applicable common stock can ever get up to a sufficiently high price so that the Warrant will have *any* value. The deeper the market slide, the deeper the pessimism, and the *lower* the Warrant will move.

This is what happened with the **R.K.O. Warrant,** which set the stage for that magnificent comeback that turned a $500 investment into $104,000, and we shall now describe how that happened. This recounting holds particular interest at this writing, because after the October 1987 market crash, hundreds of long-term Warrants were driven down to the "pennies" level, and most are still near their lows despite the recovery in many of the "blue chips" and "light blue chips." Also, the sharply lower market we expect with the inevitable onset of recession (more on this in a later chapter) will create lower and lower Warrant prices.

R.K.O. Warrants

Some years back, after some years of bad fortune, the Radio-Keith-Orpheum Co. (R.K.O.) was having difficulties meeting maturing debt and went into reorganization. As typically happens in such situations, the holders of the debt got most of the new stock in the reorganized company, while the old common stock shareholders received very little, each old share receiving only 1/16th of a share of the new common stock.

But the old common stockholders got something additional. Wishing to soften any anger (and to avoid possible lawsuits), each old common share also received one full Warrant, each Warrant representing the right to buy one share of the new R.K.O. common stock from the company itself at $15 per share, this privilege to last for five years.

(Reorganizations and mergers are a major route for the creation of new Warrants — such Warrants often being part of the "package" received by old shareholders, or the shareholders of a company being acquired.)

The logic of a long-term Warrant in the case of a reorganization is apparent, when the old shareholders receive little of the new common stock. Should the reorganized company do well in the future, the new common stock would be expected to move higher, and the Warrants could then develop value, giving the old shareholders additional compensation.

It did not start that way, however, with the new R.K.O. Warrant. Earnings of the reorganized R.K.O. continued to decline and, making matters worse, the general market headed sharply to the downside.

With all of this, the new R.K.O. common dropped down to the 2-1/2 level, and this decimated the ranks of those holders who had any hope that R.K.O. common stock would ever see the $15 level, where the Warrants would begin to develop intrinsic value. Consequently, with gloom and pessimism all about concerning R.K.O. as a company, and for the general stock market too, the

R.K.O. Warrant slid down to the *1/16* level (6-1/4 cents.)

Things rarely remain the same in the financial markets. Within a few years following the reorganization, R.K.O. earnings had turned around and were rising, and the falling market had given way to an advancing market. And, as often happens with popularly-traded low-price stocks, speculative interest was up sharply for R.K.O., and the stock was boomed up to a high of *28*.

Warrants are, above all, a matter of simple arithmetic! And "arithmetic" began to work its way with the formerly lowly R.K.O. Warrant, as the common stock headed higher.

When R.K.O. common was selling under the 15 level, the Warrant had no intrinsic value, and could sell at any low price, reflecting speculative fear or hope. But once R.K.O. common moved *above* 15, each point advance in the common added one point of exercise value to the Warrant and gave it a *minimum* value. The Warrant *had* to sell at least at that minimum price, as we explained in a previous paragraph with relation to "arbitrageurs."

What happens to a Warrant representing the right to buy common stock at *15* when the common stock is selling at *28*? Arbitrageurs are standing ready to make certain that the Warrant sells at least at the difference between 28 and 15, or *$13*, and that is exactly where the R.K.O. Warrant sold — quite a voyage from 6-1/4 cents!

We have arrived at a point which accurately spells out the inherent *leverage* of a very low-price Warrant when the common stock has a substantial recovery. Back at the low of 2-1/2 for R.K.O. common stock and 1/16 (6¼ cents) for the R.K.O. Warrant, $500 would have purchased 200 shares of the common stock, but the same $500 would have purchased **8,000 Warrants!**

And when the common stock had run up to the 28 level:

At 28 for the common, the 200
shares purchased for $500 were worth   . . . $ 5,600

But with the Warrants at $13, the
8,000 Warrants purchased for $500
were worth   . . .$104,000

The greatest Warrant opportunities come into being when the company that issued the Warrants gets *into* trouble. The common stock will fall precipitously, and the *Warrants*, which are obviously "out of the money," with pure emotion determining their price level, typically fall to very low prices — indeed, very often to the "pennies" level.

Then, if the particular Warrant situation is well-selected, the company is able to survive, and gets *out* of trouble. Often helped along by a rising stock market, the common stock can then make its way to higher price levels, while the *Warrant* will enjoy a highly-leveraged move as the common stock moves past the exercise price of the Warrant, and begins to pile up *intrinsic exercise value* for the Warrant.

Many Warrant results, in such a down-then-up cycle, produce somewhat less of a gain than what we have just described for R.K.O. Warrants, but obviously still of a greatly rewarding nature. But some moves produce an even *larger* gain. Thus, on later pages we describe what happened to the GEICO Warrant, where a $500 investment in the Warrants became worth $608,000.

Whether lesser or greater, it is clear that long-term Warrants of companies that are in trouble, should get the immediate attention of any investor looking for large-scale capital gains!

Eli Lilly Warrants

In later pages we discuss the criteria by which we judge whether a very low-price Warrant is a promising speculation. But at this time we wish to make the important point that in addition to the long-term cycle which can see a company go from trouble to better fortune, taking its low-price Warrant to spectacular heights, there are many Warrant opportunities which develop on a shorter-time scale, producing very worthwhile profits, and with other very welcome characteristics.

At the outset, let us make the statement that when a new Warrant begins trading, which Warrant originated in a merger or acquisition, with the stockholders of the company being merged or acquired having gotten *Warrants* as part of the "package," we are very likely to say "Buy automatically," in the investment service of which this writer is Editor.

The *reason* for this automatic "Buy" is that, typically, the new holders of the Warrants have only a vague idea of what Warrants are, and what their value might be, and if someone actually wants to pay money for these strange instruments, they will take it!

An excellent example of this is the **Eli Lilly Warrant,** which came into being in March 1986 when Eli Lilly acquired Hybritech, a leader in monoclonal antibody technology. Each share of Hybritech common stock was exchanged for $22 in cash and **Warrants,** each Warrant good to buy one share of Eli Lilly common stock at $75.98 per share to March 31, 1991, when the Warrants would expire. Eli Lilly is, of course, a $4 billion-in-sales manufacturer of ethical drugs, among other manufacturing divisions.

When the new Eli Lilly Warrant started trading on the New York Stock Exchange, it was at a price of *$8*, when Eli Lilly common stock was selling at *$59.25*. Consider the following Warrant "arithmetic," and remember that *most* Warrant analysis deals with the "arithmetic" of the common price, the Warrant price, the exercise price of the Warrant, and the exercise life of the Warrant. One gets very logical answers to questions in light of the mathematical relationships.

In this case, we ask the question: what would the new Eli Lilly Warrant be worth if the common were to double in price from 59.25 to 118.50? At that price, the Warrant, being the right to buy at *75.98*, has a minimum value of 118.50 minus 75.98, or *42.52*. From 8 to 42.52 is a 432% advance for the Warrant against a 100% advance in the common stock, so the Warrant would be advancing 4.32 times faster than the common stock.

But Warrants with years of life remaining almost always sell at a *premium* above actual exercise value, and it was no different with Eli Lilly Warrants. Thus, when Eli Lilly common had a run to *107.75* in early-1987, an *82%* advance from 59.25, the *Warrant* moved from that beginning level of *8* to sell at *47*, an advance of *488%*. The Eli Lilly Warrant had actually advanced *6* times faster than Eli Lilly common stock.

We have just described what happened to the Eli Lilly Warrant, in actuality, on the *up*side. What were we to expect on the *down*side when Eli Lilly Warrants were selling at 8, and the common at 59.25? While Eli Lilly was a strong performer in the marketplace and did not *sell* below 59.25, *if* it had lost 50% of its market price, to sell at 29.62, the Warrant could also have declined by 50% from 8 to 4 without showing any *greater* percentage loss. Our decades of experience in following many hundreds of Warrants tells us that the Eli Lilly Warrants, with almost 5 years of life remaining, as a "Call" on a dynamic company, would never have sold below 4 with Eli Lilly common at 29.62.

Therefore, there is no question that when Eli Lilly common was selling at 59.25 and the Warrant at 8, the Warrant had *no greater risk* than Eli Lilly common on a percentage basis on the *down*side, but in actuality did advance 6 times faster than the common stock on the *up*side. With these facts being quite indisputable, it is clear that in March 1986, with Eli Lilly common at 59.25 and the new Eli Lilly Warrants at 8, the Warrants were a *far* better buy than the common stock!

To repeat a very important point, Warrants are always a question of simple arithmetic! Utilizing that "arithmetic," let us now demonstrate that the Eli Lilly Warrants were a much better "Buy" than Eli Lilly com-

117

mon stock in March 1986, without any question, and without the need to refer to our opinion that if Eli Lilly common fell by 50%, the Warrants would show no greater percentage loss.

Assume a purchase of 100 shares of Eli Lilly common at *59.25* for $5,925.

Now assume an alternate purchase of 300 Eli Lilly Warrants at *8* for $2,400.

On the upside, we know that in the early-1987 market rise, Eli Lilly common advanced to 107.75, making the Eli Lilly Warrant (the right to buy at 75.98) worth a minimum of 42.52 on straight exercise value. We also know that with the Warrant still having four years of life remaining, the Eli Lilly Warrants were actually selling at a premium — at *47*.

The common stock, in moving from 59.25 to 107.75 in early-1987, saw the 100 shares purchased for $5,925 worth $10,775 with the common stock at 107.75, for a gain of *$4,850*.

The *Warrants*, in moving from 8 to 47, saw the 300 Warrants, purchased for $2,400, worth $14,100 with the Warrants at 47, for a gain of *$11,700*.

The great advantage of the Eli Lilly Warrant over Eli Lilly common is crystal clear:

It took a *$5,925* investment in Eli
Lilly common to produce a profit of . . . $ 4,850

While a much smaller *$2,400* investment
in Eli Lilly Warrants produced a profit of . . . $11,700

That is the *up*side. On the *down*side, even if Eli Lilly common had gone to *0*, the Warrant investment could not have shown a greater loss than the investment in the common stock. For a 50% decline in the common would have produced a loss of $2,962 in the common stock investment, while the *Warrants* with a *total* investment of *$2,400*, could have gone to *0* without showing a greater loss than the $2,962 loss in the common!

So, without resort to any opinion on our part that the Warrants would not have sold below 4 on the downside, with a 50% decline in the common, it can be categorically stated that pure logic (and pure arithmetic!) dictates that in March 1986, the Eli Lilly Warrants were a *far* better "Buy" than Eli Lilly common stock.

This makes it imperative to continuously watch the hundreds of Warrants that are trading *whenever* you are considering the purchase of a common stock. If a well-situated *Warrant* is trading for the same company, you could be throwing away extremely important advantages by not considering an investment in the Warrants, rather than the common stock.

"Hedging" With Warrants

A "Hedge" utilizing stock market instruments, usually involves being "Long" one stock market instrument and "Short" another stock market instrument, and we will be encountering this market approach in different parts of this book — with Index Options, with Convertibles, and with other instruments. Hedging with *Warrants* is particularly useful, so let us continue with the "arithmetic" already spelled out with the Eli Lilly Warrant.

Hedging aims at ensuring a substantial profit if things go well, while sharply limiting risk of loss if things do *not* go according to one's desires. "Much to gain, little to lose" characterizes a well-thought-out Hedge, and this can go so far in that welcome direction, that some Hedges can provide *only* profits and *no* losses! That, indeed, is exactly what we will see with Eli Lilly Warrants, in the Hedge position we will describe.

There is something, however, that must come first, and that "something" is an explanation of "short-selling." Few investors understand short-selling; indeed, we could say *very* few! And there is also simple prejudice against short-selling, and *fear* of short-selling among the handful of investors who do understand something about the process.

Some of the fear is justified, as we shall soon explain, but that is what makes the "Hedge" approach so welcome, since it eliminates all these fears, keeping the valuable profit-producing parts of short-selling, and mostly, or completely, getting rid of the *risk* parts.

What IS "Short-Selling"?

All investors are familiar with aiming at market profits with "long" positions, "long" meaning that you *own* the security. Thus, you buy 100 shares of General Motors common stock at, say, 50, laying out $5,000. You are "long" 100 shares of General Motors common stock. The stock runs up to 65 and you sell at that price, taking in $6,500. You paid $5,000 for the stock and sold the stock for $6,500, for a $1,500 profit. (In all of the positions we use in explaining the market behavior of Warrants, Options and Convertibles, we do not consider commissions, because they have minor effects on the outcome, and for purposes of clarity. Where commissions will have a material effect on the outcome, we deal with them separately.)

In the above example, we bought General Motors, and then we sold General Motors — quite a normal procedure. If we turn the process around and sell *first*, and *then* buy, we will have gone through a short-sale. Thus, you feel that General Motors common stock is going to decline. You call your broker and give him this order: "Sell 100 shares of General Motors common stock short, at 51 or better."

From that order, your broker knows that *you do not own* General Motors common and are selling it short, because you feel that it will go down. You also have a "limit" on your order of 51. If General Motors is selling at, say, 50, the order will not be effectuated. But if GM common goes up to that 51 level, or, hopefully, slightly above that price in a sudden rush, the order will be executed.

For every seller there is a buyer, and even though you sold 100 shares of General Motors common you did not own, the *buyer* expects to receive a certificate representing 100 shares of General Motors common stock. This is accomplished without difficulty, your broker *borrowing* that certificate from another broker, to make delivery.

Not many investors take actual delivery of their securities upon purchase, preferring to leave the certificates in the vaults of their brokerage house. Since a typical brokerage house agreement upon opening an account, gives the brokerage house the right to *lend* those certificates to another broker, this means there is typically no lack of certificates to lend, thereby making short-selling possible, which is good for the investor (making it possible to make money in *down* markets) and good for the broker (more commissions).

No harm comes to the investor whose certificate has been loaned. Any dividends paid while the certificate is out on loan are paid by the investor who sold short. His account is debited for the amount of the dividend, and the account of the investor whose certificate was loaned, is credited for the amount of the dividend. Finally, when the short-seller wishes to close out his position, the appropriate number of shares are purchased, and the certificate received with that purchase is used to replace the certificate that was loaned in the first place.

The short-sale is complete, and if the short-seller "covers his short" at a lower price than he sold short to begin with, he makes a profit. If the short-sale is covered at a *higher* price, the short-seller suffers a loss.

We now recapitulate this simple exercise in short-selling. The typical investor buys General Motors at, say, 50, and sells at, say, 60, making 10 points in profit. The *short-seller* first SELLS General Motors at 60, even though he does not own the shares, and (when fortune smiles) covers his short (BUYS) at 50, making the same 10 points in profit.

The value of short-selling is the ability to make money while a stock — or other market instrument — is *falling*, just as easily as making money while a stock is *rising*. After all, stocks do fall, as well as rise, and it is perfectly logical to attempt to make profits on the way down — just as logical, indeed, as the attempt to make profits on the way up.

We mentioned that there was *one* justified fear in short-selling, and it is this: if you *buy* General Motors common at 50, the maximum you can lose is *$50* if the stock goes to zero. On the other hand, your potential profit is unlimited, since General Motors can sell as high as fortune will take it. But if you *sell short* at 50, the potential reward is limited, while the risk of loss is *un*limited. That is, the maximum gain is 50 points (General Motors goes to 0), while there is no maximum risk of loss, since General Motors can rise to *any* price, and that portion of the rise above 50 is all loss.

We are not an enthusiast for selling short "naked," which embodies the limited gain potential, unlimited loss potential we have just described. Rather do we very much favor **Hedge** positions where the loss potential is *strictly* limited, as we shall soon see.

With all of these explanations of short-selling now behind us, we turn to an example of "Hedging with Warrants," using the same "numbers" we have already described from the action of Eli Lilly Warrants in 1986, when the Warrants commenced trading, to the subsequent 1987 high.

The Eli Lilly Common/Warrant Hedge

To first recapitulate the relevant prices, in early-March 1986, the Eli Lilly Warrant sold at *8*, while Eli Lilly common sold at *59.25*. In early 1987, the common ran up to a high of *107.75*, while the Warrants sold at a moderate premium over its actual exercise value, at *47*.

Now we assume that someone was good at analyzing the favorable situation of the Warrants, as we have already described it, and purchased 300 Eli Lilly Warrants at 8, for an outlay of $2,400. Wishing, however, to give himself more downside protection, this investor simultaneously *sold short* 100 shares of Eli Lilly common stock at 59.25.

We know the actuality of what occurred: the common ran up to 107.75, and the Warrants to 47, and here is how our "Hedge" position worked out on the upside. At 47, the 300 Warrants were worth $14,100, for a net gain of $11,700, and that is the "plus" side of our Hedge. The "minus" side was our short-sale of 100 shares at 59.25, since at *107.75*, the loss was the difference between 107.75 and 59.25, which comes to 48.50, or a loss of $4,850 on the short-sale.

Did this disturb us? Hardly. A gain of $11,700 on our "long" position in the Warrants, and a loss of $4,850 on our "short-sale," comes to an over-all net gain on the position of *$6,850*.

Not only was this a marvelous outcome for the position on the upside, but when we examine the *down*side risk in the Hedge position, the outcome shines *very* brightly! To calculate the downside potential, let us assume that Eli Lilly common drops 50% from 59.25 to *29.62*. This would mean that our short-sale of 100 shares of Eli Lilly common at 59.25 shows a profit of *$2,962*. Since the 300 Warrants in the long position had cost a *total* of *$2,400*, there was no conceivable way the Hedge position could have shown a net loss. For the short-sale gain of $2,962 was greater than the $2,400 invested in the Warrants, even if we valued the Warrants at *0*. And, obviously, they would *not* have dropped to 0!

When the Hedge position we have just described was taken in March 1986, the position *had* to show a substantial profit on the *up*side and could *not* have shown any loss on the downside.

General Tire & Rubber Warrants

To gain some additional insights into most of the points we have just made about newly-issued Warrants and hedging with Warrants, it will be quite useful to go back more than thirty years, to the example of General Tire & Rubber Warrants, thereby demonstrating that the logic and "arithmetic" of favorable Warrant situations do not change from decade to decade, but provide us with the *same* opportunities, over and over again.

In September 1956, the General Tire & Rubber Company became interested in acquiring the A.M. Byers Company, and during the course of the negotiations, the two companies found themselves still somewhat apart on what A.M. Byers' stockholders should receive for selling their shares to General Tire. General Tire's negotiators bridged the gap by adding **Warrants** to the package being offered, and this points up how many Warrants come into being in this manner, since they are a very flexible medium, allowing for the adjustment of the number of years the Warrants will run, what the exercise price would be, and how far it would be from the current common stock price on which the Warrants would be a "Call," and how many Warrants would go into the "package."

In this case, there were two classes of Warrants that were included in the final acquisition package, and the one we shall follow at this point is the Warrant that was the right to buy General Tire & Rubber common stock at *$70 per share to June 15, 1959,* and then at a slightly higher price thereafter until *June 15, 1961,* at which time the Warrants would expire. Thus, being issued in 1956, and due to expire in 1961, this was a five-year Warrant.

For all the time and effort of the negotiators of the acquisition, there were still a considerable number of original A.M. Byers' stockholders who had only a hazy idea of what a Warrant was, and sold them as fast as a market developed. Indeed, they could have asked themselves a question (they probably did), as follows: What is the good of a Warrant representing the right to buy a share of General Tire & Rubber common stock at *$70,* when I can buy that same share right now, in the open market, for *$53?*

Obviously, so many of those former A.M. Byers' shareholders asked that question, or some variety of it, that the new Warrants started trading at *4.50,* with General Tire & Rubber *common* selling at *53.* In fact, of course, all they had to do was some simple arithmetic, and to ask a very simple question: If General Tire common stock *doubles* in price, from 53 to 106, what will the new Warrant be worth? Well, when a Warrant is the right to buy at *70*, and the common is selling at *106*, the minimum value for the Warrant will be 106 minus 70, or *36*. A 100% move in the common from 53 to 106 will have produced a *700%* move in the Warrant, the Warrant moving ahead 7 times faster than the common stock.

In evaluating the worth of a Warrant, as we have just done, with the Common/Warrant prices for General Tire that then obtained, there is always a *corollary* question to ask: If the common stock *falls* by 50%, what can I expect the Warrant to sell for?

Just as with the Eli Lilly Warrant, General Tire & Rubber common did not have any appreciable decline after the Warrants started trading, but, instead, moved quite a bit higher almost immediately. So this writer has to again fall back on long experience with Warrants (which is exactly what we did in 1956, when we wrote up the new General Tire Warrants for our investment service, and recommended purchase), and our conclusion at that time was as follows: If General Tire & Rubber common declines 50%, from 53 to 26.50, the Warrant can also decline by 50%, from 4.50 to 2.25, without showing any *greater* percentage decline, and based on our experience, there is *very* little likelihood that the Warrant will sell below 2.25 as a 5-year Call on a popularly-traded stock.

As we did with the Eli Lilly Warrant, 30 years later, at the time of our earlier recommendation of the General

Tire & Rubber Warrant, we demonstrated that the Warrant was a better "Buy" than the common without any question, and without having to fall back on an opinion that the Warrant would not sell below 2.25 if the common stock fell by 50%. We did this by comparing two alternative investments, and this is something that should be done *whenever* one is analyzing a low-price Warrant, where the common stock price is a generous multiple of the Warrant price.

In this case we use the purchase of 100 shares of General Tire & Rubber common stock at 53, for $5,300, on the one hand, and *one-half* that sum, or $2,650, which buys *588* Warrants at the price the Warrants were then selling — 4.50.

A doubling in the price of the common from 53 to 106, would develop a profit of *$5,300.*

We know that at 106 for General Tire common, the Warrant, being the right to buy at *70*, has a *minimum* exercise value of 106 minus 70, or *36*. Taking that minimum price, the 588 Warrants, with the Warrants at 36, are worth *$21,168*, for a net profit of *$18,518.*

A much smaller investment in General Tire & Rubber Warrants ($2,650), had produced a *much* greater profit than the larger investment ($5,300) in the common!

Going further, to drive this *very* important point home, if, instead of doubling in price, General Tire common had done *down,* to lose half its value at 26.50, the investment of $5,300 in 100 shares would show a loss of *$2,650.* But the investment of $2,650 in 588 Warrants could drop to *zero*, and show no greater loss than the common!

So the conclusion was as inescapable in 1956 with the General Tire common/Warrant relationship, as it was 30 years later with the Eli Lilly common/Warrant relationship. The Warrants *had* to be a better "Buy" than the common, because it would provide a much greater profit than the common if the common moved *higher*, but could not show a greater loss than the common if the common moved *lower*.

And, of course, we know that since the Warrants, in both cases, would *not* go to zero, the Warrants would show a *smaller* loss on the downside, further accentuating their large advantage.

It is useful at this point to demonstrate that just as the Eli Lilly Warrants were amenable to a *Hedge* position, the General Tire & Rubber Warrants possessed exactly the same potential advantage for those investors who understood "short-selling" and what could be accomplished with a Warrant/common Hedge.

As we explained at the time, consider a $2,250 investment in 500 General Tire & Rubber Warrants at 4.50, and a simultaneous Hedge position, which entailed selling short 100 shares of General Tire common at 53, for $5,300.

If we now envisage that doubling in price of the common from 53 to 106, we would have generated a $5,300 paper *loss* in the short-sale.

But, as we have already seen, at 106 for General Tire common, the *Warrants*, being the right to buy at *70*, have a minimum exercise value of *36*, whereupon our 500 Warrants are worth $18,000, and when we deduct the $2,250 we paid for the Warrants, our net profit is *$15,750.*

A gain of $15,750 on the Warrants versus a loss of $5,300 on the common short-sale, and we have a net profit of *$10,450.* The Hedge had worked its magic on the upside!

On the *down*side, assume again a 50% decline in the common from 53 to 26.50, and our short-sale of the common would have produced a *profit* of $2,650: that is what short-sales *do* on a decline. This means that the $2,250 we invested in the 500 Warrants at 4.50 have *complete protection*, because the gain on the short-sale of the common ($2,650) is greater than our entire investment in the Warrants ($2,250). There is no way we can show a loss on the downside.

In point of fact, since the Warrants would *not* be selling at 0, but probably at least at the $2 figure with the common at 26.50, there would be a goodly net *profit* with the Hedge position on the downside. Which leads us to the happy conclusion that such a Hedge position would show a profit both on the upside *and* the downside! And the same thing would hold true for the Eli Lily Warrant that we previously described, and many other common/Warrant relationships at different stages of the stock market cycle.

Wrapping Up The History Of The
General Tire & Rubber Warrants

Following what we have just described for General Tire & Rubber Warrants, the fact that the common and Warrants subsequently had a big run to the upside highlights the very large importance of the potential of a Hedge position which *eliminated* downside risk.

For understanding how to utilize the Hedge would surely have permitted a larger investment in the Warrants than would have been prudent *without* the Hedge. Indeed, the Hedge converted a speculation into an investment! And the payoff would have been very large when General Tire & Rubber common soared from 53 to the equivalent of 280 (adjusting for stock splits, with the Warrant exercise terms being adjusted along with the common). If the common soared, the Warrants *exploded*, moving from 4.50 to 210, advancing *much* faster than the common stock.

There were two other General Tire & Rubber Warrants that deserve mention. One was a "$60" Warrant, which had been issued at the same time as the Warrant we have been discussing in depth. This Warrant rose from 7.25 to 215. And a "$25" Warrant had a run from 5 to a high of 90, at a slightly later date. Throughout this period of advancing prices for General Tire & Rubber common, all three series of Warrants were able to *far* outstrip the move in the common stock, making possible the superior leverage we have described, along with the potential for Hedge positions, which heightened the appeal of the Warrants to a *great* degree.

Profound LOSSES With Warrants
As Well As Gains!

We will shortly be describing some of the many ways in which Warrants come into existence, using a prolific period in 1986-1987 for our examples, when a rising market caused a string of Warrant success stories. And some pages later we will be returning to the reality of high-leverage Warrants when *huge* successes can reward well-timed Warrant purchases through a cycle of a company that gets *into* trouble, and then gets *out* of trouble. Along those lines, we will be spelling out how this happened with GEICO Warrants, where a $500 investment became worth $608,000.

As an "antidote" to all these success stories, and to drive home a very important point that *there are many more losses with Warrants than gains* (otherwise, how could we get all those very low-price Warrants which makes all those success stories possible?), let us bring to the reader's attention some notable *losses* that have occurred with Warrants in past markets.

Atlantic Richfield Warrants Disappear
Into A Black Hole

In mid-1969, the then oil giant, Cities Service Company, wanted to sell an issue of $100,000,000 in bonds, a *very* large issue at that time. Wishing to ensure a successful sale, and one with a lower interest rate for the bonds, the company turned to a block of 500,000 shares of Atlantic Richfield Oil common stock which it had accumulated, and decided to use it to back *Warrants* that it would issue in conjunction with the bonds. This was an approach that had been used previously, and would be used again — even to the period in which we are writing.

Thus, the purchaser of Cities Service bonds got five Warrants with each $1,000 face value of bond, each Warrant good to buy one share of Atlantic Richfield common stock, *from Cities Service*, upon payment of $110 per share. Thus, Atlantic Richfield itself, as a company, had nothing to do with this issue, the common stock to satisfy any exercise of these Warrants coming from *Cities Service's* holdings of Atlantic Richfield common stock.

As stated in the Bonds-plus-Warrants Prospectus for the issue, the exercise privilege at $110 per share would expire on September 1, 1972, making this a three-year Warrant.

The managers of the $100,000,000 bond issue were proved correct in their thinking that adding the Warrants would make the sale an easy one, with better terms for Cities Service, as the complete issue sold out quickly. One thing to keep in mind is that even though Cities Service had *issued* the Warrants, the future course of the Warrants, which were traded separately after the Bond-plus-Warrants issue was publicly sold, had to do only with what was happening to **Atlantic Richfield** common stock, and not with Cities Service.

Along these lines, Atlantic Richfield common stock moved sharply higher after the Warrants came on the market, the common boiling up to a 118 top, which caused excited speculators to pay *47.25* for those Warrants at that top for the common stock. This reminds us that Warrants can be both *under*valued, as we saw with General Tire & Rubber Warrants, and Eli Lilly Warrants, and *over*valued, as we shall now describe for the then newly-trading Atlantic Richfield Warrants, constituting a sharp reminder that all Warrants are not an easy road to riches. Far from it!

The speculators who paid 47.25 for the Atlantic Richfield Warrants when the Atlantic Richfield common stock was selling at 118, did not have very exciting prospects on the upside, as some quick analysis would have demonstrated.

Thus, assume a 50% advance in the common from 118 to 177, whereupon the Warrants, the right to buy at *110*, would have an exercise value of 177 minus 110, or *67.* Once again drawing upon our experience with many hundreds of Warrants, we would estimate that at that point, the Warrants would probably sell at a premium above exercise value of about 10 points, bringing the Warrants to a price of about 77.

But 77 would be only a 63% advance from 47.25, little more than the 50% advance in Atlantic Richfield common. Not only would this be a result hardly worth aiming at, but on the *down*side, the Warrants would decline much faster than the common. The Atlantic Richfield Warrant was distinctly overvalued at 47.25, in relation to the 118 price of the common stock. And this was particularly true when taking into consideration the 3-year life of the Warrant, since Cities Service had not been generous in this regard.

What subsequently happened to the Warrants served to emphasize the *large* risks inherent in them at their inflated levels. Atlantic Richfield common stock went into a slump, which was accentuated in the 1972 market decline. The common stock never again got near that 110 level, and the Warrants moved steadily lower until expiration date in September 1972 rolled around, whereupon the Warrant expired at — *zero.*

At the 47.25 top, the Atlantic Richfield Warrants — 500,000 in number — had a market value of *$23,625,000,* and *all* that value disappeared into nothingness when expiration date arrived, with the common selling well below the exercise price of 110.

Meanwhile, what about Cities Service that had enjoyed the ease of selling its $100,000,000 bond issue because of the attached Warrants? They still had their 500,000 shares of Atlantic Richfield common stock. Theoretically, they could have sold Warrants on their Atlantic Richfield holdings again!

This all serves to demonstrate that (a) Warrants are very definitely a two-way street, and (b) each Warrant situation must be analyzed carefully to demonstrate its potential gain on the upside, and its downside risks. A Warrant holding is *not* favorable unless it fulfills that welcome description: "Much more to gain on the upside than to lose on the downside."

We shall run into that prescription in many other chapters that follow.

The Evaluation Of A Warrant

Over many years of following hundreds of Warrants, we have found the following "formula" to be quite helpful in determining whether a Warrant, given the existing market price for Warrant and common, is overvalued, undervalued, or "fairly" valued. The following steps are involved:

1. Assume a 50% advance in the common stock.

2. Assume *another* 50% advance in the common stock.

3. Asssume, after the second 50% advance for the common, that the Warrant is selling for its straight *exercise value.*

4. Take one-half of that exercise value.

5. Now take one-half of what resulted from Step (4).

At this point you have the *existing* "fair value" for the Warrant, and you compare it to the price at which the Warrant is actually selling. If the Warrant is selling well below the "fair value," it is undervalued. If it is selling quite close to the "fair value," it is fully priced. If it is selling well above the "fair value," it is overvalued.

Remember now that when the Eli Lilly Warrant started trading around the 8 level, with Eli Lilly common selling at 59.25, each Warrant could be exchanged for one share of common stock upon payment of $75.98 until March 31, 1991, when the Warrant would expire. Following the above formula, and taking the beginning prices for Eli Lilly common and Warrants, we now:

(1) Assume a 50% advance for Eli Lilly common from 59.25 to 88.875.

(2) Assume a *second* 50% advance from 88.875 to 133.31.

(3) The Eli Lilly Warrant being the right to buy at 75.98, we deduct 75.98 from 133.31 to arrive at an exercise value of *57.33*.

(4) One-half of that 57.33 exercise value is 28.66.

(5) One-half of 28.66 is *14.33*, which is the "fair value" of the Eli Lilly Warrant, with the common at 59.25 and an exercise right at 75.98.

But the Eli Lilly Warrant was selling at *8*. It was considerably undervalued and, therefore, proceeded to far outstrip Eli Lilly common on the upside, while, at the same time, protecting capital on the *down*side.

Asarco '91 Warrants

In the 5-29-89 issue of the **R.H.M. Survey of Warrants, Options & Low-Price Stocks**, we find Asarco common stock selling at 28-7/8 and the Asarco Warrant selling at 12-7/8. Asarco is a leading producer of copper, silver, lead and zinc, among other operations, and the Warrant represents the right to buy one share of Asarco common stock for $16.09, this privilege to last to August 15, 1991, when the Warrant will expire.

Given these figures, is the Warrant undervalued, overvalued or somewhere in-between?

Following the formula:

(1) We multiply 28.875 by 1.5 (a 50% advance) and get 43.31.

(2) We multiply 43.31 by 1.5 and get 64.97.

(3) We deduct the exercise price (16.09) from 64.97 and get 48.88, which is the straight exercise value of the Warrant.

(4) We take one-half of that exercise value and get 24.44.

(5) We take one-half of the result in (4) and get *12.22*, and *that* is the fair value for the Asarco Warrant when the common is at 28-7/8. Since the Warrant was *selling* at 12-7/8, and the fair value was 12.22, the Warrant could be termed "fairly valued."

We can make the point that even at its "fairly-valued" price, the Asarco Warrant still promised to advance twice as fast as Asarco common. That is, Asarco common goes from 28.875 to 43.31, up 50%, while the Asarco Warrant goes from 12.875 to 24.44, not much less than 100%.

It is not enough, however, to calculate what the Warrant will do on the *up*side. What if Asarco *declines* by 50% from 28.875 to 14.43? Will the Asarco Warrant also decline only by 50% from 12.875 to 6.44? We do not think so. We feel we would more likely find the Asarco Warrant selling closer to, say, the *4* level, possibly lower.

What conclusion should we draw from this? The conclusion would be that a *fairly-valued Warrant* is still likely to advance about twice as fast as the common stock on the upside, but is *also* likely to *decline* considerably faster than the common stock, on a percentage basis. Given that prospect, one could not say in May 1989 that the Asarco Warrant was an attractive purchase.

This does not mean that this state of affairs would never change. There could be a profound market downswing and/or a sharp decline for Asarco common stock itself, whereupon the Asarco Warrant might reach quite low levels and the "numbers" could then proclaim it an opportunity for a leveraged gain. And this same possibility is true for a *long list* of Warrants that cannot currently be deemed attractive for purchase. Warrant/common price relationships are in a continuous state of flux, and require constant evaluation.

Southwest Airlines Warrants

A very important first step in considering the potential of a Warrant is also a very *simple* one: Divide the common price by the Warrant price. If you get a *low* number, the Warrant is not likely to represent a purchase opportunity. If you get a *high* number, the Warrant has passed its first test of being attractive for purchase.

Note that when the Eli Lilly Warrant was selling at 8, while the common was selling at 59.25, dividing 59.25 by 8 gave us a result of *7.4*. That is a high number as Warrant/common ratios go. And the Eli Lilly Warrant did indeed prove to be an attractive Warrant.

Where the *Asarco* Warrant was concerned, however, we get quite a different answer. With Warrant and common selling at 12.875 and 28.875 respectively, dividing 28.875 by 12.875 gives us a result of *2.2*. That is a very low ratio, and it is to be expected that in our analysis of the Warrant, we came up with the conclusion that it was *not* attractive for purchase.

After the October 1987 market crash, hundreds of Warrants dropped down to very low prices, many under the $1 level, and even though a substantial market recovery has been going on, this has been evidenced mostly in the blue chips and the more important secondary stocks.

So it is not surprising that hundreds of Warrants *still* languish at low levels. *Further*, Warrants without intrinsic value (selling out of the money) reflect mostly the emotional state of investors, and really bullish feelings have not, up to this writing, made themselves evident.

It, therefore, being very important to understand the leverage potential of very low-price Warrants, let us consider the **Southwest Airlines Warrant** when it was selling at 1/4 (25 cents), in September 1988, with the common stock at 17.25, and the Warrant representing the right to buy a share of common stock at 35.00 to 6-25-90.

Obviously, when we divide 17.25 by .25 we are going to get a high number, and that indeed was the case, the ratio being 69!

At this point let us also use our previously-explained "formula" to determine the valuation of the Southwest Airlines Warrant at the prices given for Warrant and common.

(1) We multiply 17.25 by 1.5 and get 25.875.

(2) We multiply 25.875 by 1.5 and get 38.81.

(3) We deduct the exercise price (35.00) from 38.81, and get 3.81, which is the straight exercise value of the Warrant when the common is at 38.81.

(4) We take one-half of the exercise value, and get 1.90.

(5) Finally, we take one-half of the result in (4) and get *95 cents*, which is the fair value of the Warrant when the common is at 17.25, as it was in September 1988.

With the fair value at 95 cents, the Warrant selling at *25* cents, and with the common stock selling at a very *large* multiple of the Warrant, all the guidelines say that the Southwest Airlines Warrant was an excellent speculation.

To demonstrate that there is *much else* that goes into recognizing a Warrant opportunity, we will be recounting some of the points we made in an extended report we did on the company and the Warrant in the **R.H.M Survey** of January 6, 1989, when the Warrant was selling at *50 cents* and the common stock was selling at *$20.00*.

To begin with, *Group Movement* is a very important factor in the stock market, and for Warrants, Scores and Convertibles, it is vital to be aware of this phenomenon.

Thus, if, for example, automobile stocks are trending lower, as evidenced by their Group chart, one cannot expect too much from a stock associated with automobiles. On the other hand, if *oil* stocks are dominating the financial news in a dramatic across-the-board rise, Warrants for an oil company's stock — or Scores, or Convertibles for an oil company's stock — would all deserve our concentrated interest.

(Note: in the *"Current Supplement"* offered to readers of this book, without charge, there is an updated listing by *Group* of all currently trading Warrants, Scores and Convertibles, and this is a valuable market tool. Information about securing this Current Supplement, which also includes other updated information, is given in a few places in this book.)

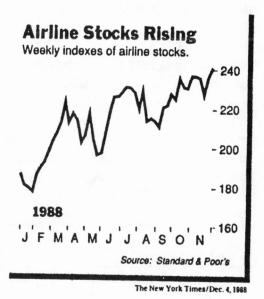

Airline Stocks Rising
Weekly indexes of airline stocks.

Source: Standard & Poor's

The New York Times/Dec. 4, 1988

The chart shown (courtesy of the **New York Times**) was presented in our 1-6-89 write-up on Southwest Airlines Warrants, and the bullish trend for Airline stocks is quite evident, further adding to the speculative potential of the Warrant.

In considering any Warrant investment, understanding the *fundamentals* of the company that issued the Warrants, is just as important as the statistical evaluation of the Warrant, as we have just described it.

In the case of Southwest Airlines, the long-term price chart shown on the next page (courtesy of **Standard &**

143

Poor's) portrays the common stock moving to the downside in zig-zag fashion since the 35-1/4 high made in 1983.

Formerly a Texas intrastate airline, Southwest Airlines has grown in recent years through expanding its route system. The company did stumble in one acquisition — Muse Air — but liquidated the mistake, and went on to expand its market areas. However, it avoided the mistake of *over*expanding. At the present time, its largest three markets are Houston, Dallas and Phoenix, with San Antonio, Chicago, Albuquerque and Austin

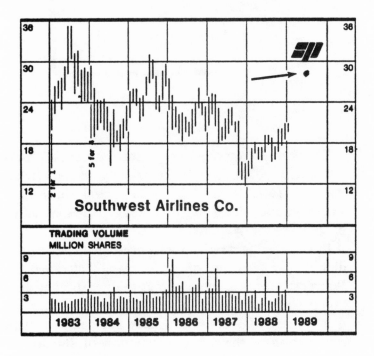

Southwest Airlines Co.

TRADING VOLUME
MILLION SHARES

constituting the next four markets with greatest contributions to revenues.

The strength of Southwest Airlines, as we saw it in our report, was its policy of point-to-point scheduling of aircraft, which aims at serving the local short-flight business traveler much more conveniently than the "hub-and-spoke" approach of most other airlines. This has enabled the company to offer a large number of convenient daily departures between nonstop city pairs, with an outstanding on-time performance record.

The result has been that Southwest's cost per seat-mile, as recently reported, is 5.73 cents, which is 25% less than the average for large carriers. For 1988, Operating Revenues went up 10.5%, but Net Income per common share went up *187%*, to $1.84 per share, while analysts familiar with the company's operations are looking for 1989 to produce earnings of about $2.20 per share, which will be an all-time record high for earnings as, indeed, the 1988 result was as well.

These are some of the "fundamentals" that go into any company analysis, and our analysis of Southwest Airlines for the **R.H.M. Survey** went considerably further than the above-described factors, with the conclusion being reached that the Warrants were a "Buy." 1989 was very kind to Southwest Airlines common stock — with the airlines also continuing to move higher as a Group — and a high of 28-3/4 was reached (our arrow on the chart shows this high), while the *Warrants* were reaching a high of *1-3/4*.

Let us now consider the leverage enjoyed by the Warrant over the common stock. Recall that in September

1988, the common stock of Southwest Airlines was selling at *17-1/4*, while the Warrants were selling at *1/4*. From 17-1/4 to the 1989 high (thus far) of 28-3/4 represented an advance of *67%*, while the advance in the Warrants from 1/4 to 1-3/4 represented an advance of *600%*. The Warrant had advanced *9 times* faster than the common stock.

How The Time Factor Fits Into Our Equation

Thus far in our "Evaluation" of Warrants, we have ignored the length of life still remaining for exercise. Obviously, this *is* a very important factor, but we excluded it for the moment, to get our major point across. Where the Southwest Airlines Warrant is concerned, we *must* now take seriously the fact that it is due to *expire* on June 25, 1990. When we recommended purchase in January of 1989, it still had about 18 months of life remaining, but as we are writing, this is down to slightly less than one year.

Our experience has been, where our Evaluation Equation is concerned, that if Warrants have more than two years of exercise life remaining, the "time" question has only marginal influence, and we can take the conclusion of the "Equation" without hesitation.

Once we get *under* the two-year mark, we should "shade" our results to some small extent, and once we get under the 18-month mark, we should use the Evaluation Equation only as a very rough guide, giving greater weight to other factors.

In the case of Southwest Airlines Warrants (and many

other Warrants in the same "very low-price" category) one of the most important factors is the low price itself! Thus, when you have a Warrant at 1/4, how far down can it go? Obviously — 1/4, and no more. When a Warrant still has more than about a year to run, with the common stock at a high multiple of the Warrant — and this was certainly true of Southwest Airlines — the "Equation" is less important than the low price, and if the common stock begins to move, a leveraged move by the Warrant is certain.

If we look at the Southwest Airlines situation as we are writing, with one year of exercise life remaining, the Warrant being the right to buy at *35.00*, what shall we think of the further speculative potential of the Warrant, when it is selling at 1.31, while the common is at 25.50?

To begin with, *much* depends on the general market. At this writing, the Dow Jones Industrial Average has surpassed the 2500 level, the bond market is strong, the dollar is strong, and the stock market could "bubble" further to the upside.

Group Movement continues to be an important indicator, and the latest Group chart for the Airlines (see next page — courtesy of **Securities Research**) continues the lively upswing discussed on an earlier page. Further, take note of the *Relative Strength Line* for the Air Transport Group, directly under the Air Transport name, indicating that the Air Transport Group is *outperforming* the rest of the market.

Even with all these positive signs, the dwindling time value of the Warrant *must* be given full weight. The

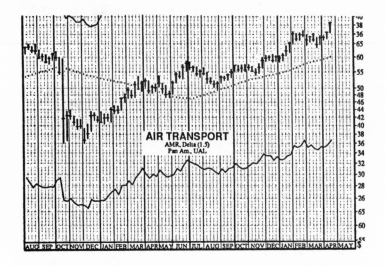

common stock has to make it up to the 35 level before June 1990, to give the Southwest Airlines Warrant intrinsic value, and that is still quite a distance from 25.50. Consequently, our approach in this instance would be to recommend very *modest* commitments at current levels, but to make additional purchases *on a scale down*.

For example, a market "correction" to the downside at this point could easily knock the Warrant down to the 1 level, and even 3/4, and good potential for a trading profit could then have been created.

Thus, the time factor with Warrants *is* of the utmost importance, but with very low-price Warrants, it is considerably less important than with high-price Warrants, where diminution of time value has *large* effects. When dealing with the *hundreds* of Warrants selling under the $1 level as we are writing, all the above factors must be kept constantly in mind.

Learning From Individual Warrants

If we look at how a number of Warrants have acted recently, we will get additional insight into:

(a) why and how Warrants are issued by various companies;

(b) what we can expect for the market action of such Warrants, and

(c) when such Warrants are excellent profit opportunities, and when they should be avoided.

Capital Cities/ABC Warrants

It is quite appropriate (and educational!) that we should go from discussing a Warrant selling at 1/4 (the earlier price of the Southwest Airlines Warrant) to a Warrant selling initially in the $30 range!

Also, there is the great contrast between a Southwest Airlines Warrant being the right to buy stock at *$35* per share, and a Capital Cities/ABC Warrant being the right to buy stock at *$250* per share. Since we, at different times, recommended that both should be purchased, it is evident that Warrant "arithmetic" works in *any* price range.

In March 1985, American Broadcasting Companies ("ABC") was merged into Capital Cities Communications, the new entity being known as Capital Cities/ABC. We have already seen that both Eli Lilly Warrants and General Tire & Rubber Warrants came into being as a result of *mergers* in which stockholders of the companies being acquired received *Warrants* as part of the acquisition "package."

We also had made the point in both cases that when Warrants are received by such stockholders, *they should almost always be bought as soon as they begin trading*, because the Warrants are completely unfamiliar to most investors, and they proceed to sell them at prices which typically later prove to be *bargain* prices. This is true *whenever* stockholders receive Warrants because of a merger, acquisition, or some other financial event.

It was no different with ABC stockholders when they received Warrants as part of the acquisition package from Capital Cities Communications. Each Warrant (and there were 2.85 million of those Warrants) represented the right to buy one share of the newly-combined companies — Capital Cities/ABC — for $250 — the Warrants to expire on July 29, 1988. Thus, it was only a two year Warrant.

In the **R.H.M. Survey** of 4-18-86, we find the new Capital Cities/ABC Warrant with a "Buy" recommendation, the Warrants selling at *30.50*, and the common stock selling at *228.50*. Here is what our "Evaluation Equation" told us:

Divide the common price by the Warrant price (228.50 divided by 30.50), and we get *7.49*, which is a number sufficiently high to mark the Warrant as worth looking into as a purchase, from that initial criterion.

We then apply our Evaluation Equation, as follows:

(1) We multiply 228.5 by 1.5 and get 342.75.

(2) We multiply 342.75 by 1.5 and get 514.13.

(3) We deduct the exercise price of the Warrant (250) from 514.13 and get 264.13, which is the straight exercise value of the Warrant when the common is at 514.13.

(4) We take one-half of the exercise value, and get 132.06.

(5) Finally, we take one-half of the result in (4) and get *66.03*, which is the fair value of the Warrant when the common is at 228.50, as it was in April 1986.

So the Capital Cities/ABC Warrant was selling at *30.50* when its fair value was *66.03*. That is *quite* an undervaluation, and demonstrates again how new Warrants resulting from mergers and acquisitions, very often start trading at bargain levels because the stockholders who received the Warrants have little comprehension of their true long-term value.

Capital Cities Communications, after acquiring American Broadcasting Companies, had become a media giant, revenues jumping from $1 billion to $4 billion as the newspapers, shopping guides and myriad other publications were added to the television and radio networks of ABC.

In subsequent years, the fine outlook for the combined companies was demonstrated by strong earnings gains, jumping from $11.20 per share in 1986 to $16.46 per share in 1987, and to $22.31 per share in 1988. The common stock of the new Capital Cities/ABC proceeded to move sharply higher, as shown on the chart (see the following page — chart courtesy of **Securities Research**).

Prior to the October 1987 market break, the common stock reached *450*, and the Warrant, being the right to buy at 250, sold at its exercise value of *200*. The reason for the lack of a premium over exercise value was that the Warrant had only a 2-year life to begin with, and by its 1987 high, the exercise life was already less than one year. Furthermore, *high-priced* Warrants — and 200 is a *high* price (!) — always sell at lower premiums over exercise value than do *lower-priced* Warrants.

From the April 1986 prices, the common stock had advanced from 228.50 to 450.00, an advance of *97%*, while the Warrants had advanced from 30.50 to 200.00, an advance of *556%*. Illustrating the fact that high-priced Warrants can act very much like low-priced Warrants do, when both are favorably situated, recall that the Southwest Airlines Warrant had advanced *600%* while the Capital Cities/ABC Warrant had advanced *555%*, as we have just recounted.

CAPITAL CITIES/ABC, INC. (CCB)

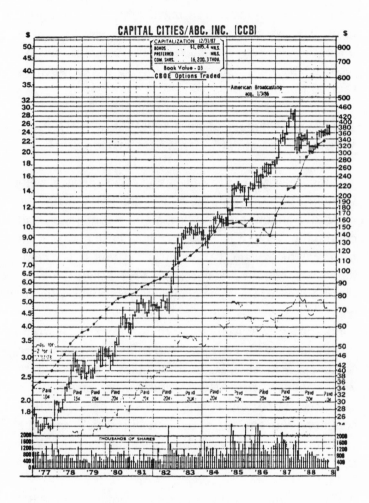

And what has also been demonstrated once again is the likelihood of a new Warrant, emanating from a merger or an acquisition, selling at a very attractive price in the early stages of its trading activity when it comes upon the market. This has led us to almost always recommend immediate purchase of such Warrants, as soon as trading begins.

The Clear Advantage of the Capital Cities/ABC Warrant Over Capital Cities/ABC Common Stock

It is necessary to fully understand *how* superior a well-situated Warrant can be, when compared with the respective common stock, because in recent years, and continuing through to this day, there have always been *hundreds* of Warrants trading, and if you buy a common stock without first checking to see if there is a Warrant trading for the same company, you might willingly embrace some *severe* disadvantages.

So, just as we went through the relevant Warrant "arithmetic" with **Eli Lilly Warrants** and **General Tire & Rubber Warrants,** let us review that same procedure with **Capital Cities/ABC** to add further emphasis to these very important concepts. We are dealing with a common/Warrant price relationship which saw the common stock go from 228.50 to 450.00, and the Warrant go from 30.50 to its straight exercise value of 200.00.

If we had purchased 100 shares of Capital Cities/ABC common stock at 228.50, we would have expended *$22,850*, and when the common advanced to 450, the

100 shares were worth *$45,000,* for a gain of *$22,150.*

Alternatively, if we purchased 350 Capital Cities/ABC *Warrants* at 30.50 (the market price of the Warrants when the common was at 228.50), we would have expended *$10,675,* and when the Warrants advanced to 200.00 (their straight exercise value), the 350 Warrants were worth *$70,000,* for a gain of *$59,325.*

$22,850 invested in the common stock had produced a profit of *$22,150*;

while less than half that amount, or *$10,675* invested in the Warrants had produced a profit of *$59,325.*

The Capital Cities/ABC Warrants were *far* ahead of the common stock on the upside. But what about the *down*side? Suppose the advantage of the Warrant on the *up*side was offset by poor performance on the *down*side. We know, of course, that this will not be so, from our former examples of Eli Lilly Warrants and General Tire & Rubber Warrants, and when we go through the relevant "arithmetic," that is exactly what we find.

If the common stock of Capital Cities/ABC lost half its value, from 228.50 to 114.25, there would be a loss of *$11,425.*

Since the *entire investment* in the Capital Cities/ABC Warrants was $10,675, there could *not* be a *greater* loss for the Warrants than the common, even if the Warrants had gone to zero! But our estimate is that with the common at 114.25, the Warrants would be selling at about the *15* level, or a 15.5 loss on 350 Warrants, which comes to *$5,425*.

So on the downside, we find a loss of *$10,675* for the common stock, but only *$5,425* for the Warrants.

Upside or downside, an investment in the Capital Cities/ABC Warrants, when they were selling at 30.5, was a *far* better investment than Capital Cities/ABC common stock. And this again emphasizes that with hundreds of Warrants trading, and new Warrants steadily coming on the scene, *always* check the Warrant list *whenever* you are considering the purchase of a common stock.

A Common/Warrant Hedge Position With Capital Cities/ABC

We trust that in previous pages we have led the reader to be more accepting of the concept (and the practice!) of *short-selling*. With Hedge positions, indeed, short-selling should be completely acceptable because it contributes to sharply-reduced risk, or even the absence of risk (!), as we shall soon demonstrate once again.

What makes even investors with some knowledge of short-selling justifiably nervous about that market maneuver is the following: If you *buy* a security, the maximum loss is what you paid for the security. But if you sell a security short, there *is* no maximum, for there is no limit, theoretically, to the increase in price which a security can attain. And to the extent that the shorted security goes *up*, your *loss* goes up.

For example, you *buy* 100 shares of ABC Inc. common stock at 50, laying out $5,000. The maximum loss you can sustain is — $5,000 — which assumes ABC common has gone to zero. The loss cannot be any greater.

Now, instead, you *sell 100 shares of ABC common short*, at 50. If ABC common now goes to *100*, and you cover your short, you have a loss of $5,000. That is, you took in $5,000 when you sold the stock short, and must pay $10,000 to buy 100 shares of ABC common at 100 to replace the stock you sold short at 50, to terminate the position.

If ABC common goes to *200*, you have a loss of $15,000, if to *300*, a loss of $25,000. It is all open-ended. Theoretically, your potential loss is *unlimited*. And it is that open-ended possibility of loss with a short-sale that correctly frightens investors.

Now observe how short-selling Capital Cities/ABC common stock not only does not threaten you with open-ended loss, but actually eliminates possible loss! Recall that Capital Cities/ABC is selling at 228.50 and the Warrant is selling at 30.50. Each Capital Cities/ABC Warrant is the right to buy the common stock at $250 per share.

We now set up the following Hedge position:

(A) We *buy* 350 Capital Cities/ABC Warrants at 30.50, laying out *$10,675*.

(B) We *sell short* 100 shares of Capital Cities/ABC common stock at 228.50, taking in *$22,850*.

We know that in actuality, Capital Cities/ABC common stock ran up to *450* in 1987, so the 100 shares we sold short at 228.50 would show a loss of $45,000 minus $22,850, or a loss of *$22,150*.

But, at 450 for the common stock, the Capital Cities/ABC *Warrant*, being the right to buy common at 250, must sell at a minimum of *200*, and that is where it actually sold. Our 350 Warrants, purchased at 30.50 for $10,675, are now worth 350 x 200 or $70,000.

Deduct $10,675 from $70,000, and our gain is *$59,325*.

Gain of *$59,325* on the long position in the Warrants, and loss of *$22,150* on the short position in the common stock, and our *net gain* is *$37,175*.

And no matter how high Capital Cities/ABC common might go, because we were short *100* shares, and long *350* shares via the Warrants, our net profit would have to climb higher and higher, because the net position was actually long 250 shares of common stock.

CURRENT SUPPLEMENT AVAILABLE

As this book was going to press, important developments were taking place. Long-Term *Warrants* on dozens of the most important Japanese companies, already trading in Europe, will, before too long, trade in the United States as well.

Stock Index *Futures* and Stock Index *Options* on the Japanese stock markets are already trading in Japan and elsewhere, and are preparing to trade in the United States. They will be highly-important speculative mediums, along the lines set forth in this book.

In the **Current Supplement,** the latest approaches to Index Option speculation are described, in light of the most recent stock market action.

In addition, the Current Supplement contains a valuable alphabetical listing by *Industry Group*, of all Warrants, Convertibles and Scores trading today, plus other current information important in today's market, regarding these fields.

The publishers of this book would like to send you this Current Supplement. Just send your name and address to:

Current Supplement, Department 96
R.H.M. Press
172 Forest Avenue
Glen Cove, New York 11542

There is no cost or obligation.

The Downside

If Capital Cities common went to *zero*, our short-sale of 100 shares at 228.50, for $22,850 would, of course, result in a *profit* of *$22,850*. Since the entire cost of our long position in 350 Warrants was *$10,675*, our net gain would have to be *$12,175*.

Now, to make a more reasonable assumption, say that Capital Cities/ABC common went down *50%*, from 228.50 to 114.25. We would have a gain of *$11,425* on our short position in 100 shares common at 228.50. Since this amount is still larger than the total investment in 350 Warrants — $10,675 — *there could be no net loss on the position*. But since it is reasonable, from experience, that with the common at 114.25, the Warrants should sell at about *15*, the actual loss in the Warrants would be 15.5 points on 350 Warrants, or $5,425.

In this instance, gain of *$11,425* on the short-sale of 100 shares common, and loss of *$5,425* on the long position in 350 Warrants, and our *net gain* would be *$6,000*.

Conclusion

The Hedge position we have just outlined of short Capital Cities/ABC common stock, and long Capital Cities/ABC Warrants, *had* to show a substantial profit whether Capital Cities/ABC common stock went up *or* down!

There are several very important additional factors to consider here. When you sell a security short, *you do not have to put up any funds* to accomplish the transaction. All short-sales are automatically accomplished in a "margin account," and if you are carrying fully-paid securities in that margin account (if needed, fully-paid securities can simply be switched from your "cash" account to a "margin account"), in excess of the size of the short-sale, that would satisfy the requirements for selling short and would not require you to put up any additional funds at the inception of the position.

Therefore, you might own General Motors common stock, or Treasury securities, or any other security, and if these are reposing in your margin account, they are not affected in any manner, but they serve the purpose of allowing you to take short positions without putting up additional funds.

Thus, the *net profit* that eventuates is a very high return on the actual cash invested, because the only portion that required putting up cash is the long position in the 350 Warrants.

That being so, if that Warrant long position involved *$10,675* (350 Warrants at 30.50), a gain of *$37,175* on the upside, or *$6,000* on the downside, would be a *very large* percentage profit on the actual cash involved, and earned without risk! Even on more modest moves in a Warrant/common Hedge position than we have just described for Capital Cities/ABC, the net return would *still* be riskless and large.

Therefore, when a Warrant is selling at a favorable price in relation to the common, along the lines we have been discussing with Eli Lilly, General Tire & Rubber and Capital Cities/ABC, think seriously about setting up the type of Hedge position we have just described. We are fully aware that the vast majority of investors do *not* like to sell short, and find "Hedge" positions "too complicated," but we trust we have demonstrated that the potential rewards are so large, and the diminution or elimination of risk so welcome, that the reader should overcome those fears and prejudices!

Another Factor Enters Our Warrant Evaluation Equation

Thus far we have seen that the *time* factor (exercise life still remaining), must often be considered with our Warrant Evaluation Equation, which tells us what the "fair value" of a Warrant is, so that this price may be compared with the current price of a Warrant in which we may have an interest.

Now we enter another area which is at least equally important — the anticipated *volatility* of the common stock price, and the time frame for the profit horizons for the company itself. These additional factors do not take anything away from what the Equation can provide for us in the way of guidance; they *add* to the value of the guidance. What follows will also introduce the reader to the type of *analyses of fundamentals* which are an indispensable part of arriving at the value of a Warrant.

Equitable Resources Warrants

This major point is well illustrated by looking at **Equitable Resources Warrants** as we are writing. We remind readers at this point that every one of our discussions about individual Warrants, as presented in these pages, adds significantly to the reader's understanding of how Warrants operate, and what can be accomplished with them where capital growth is concerned.

Equitable Resources Warrants came into being on June 24, 1987, as illustrated by the newspaper advertisement of the time (see next page) and reminding us that one of the most common avenues for origination of Warrant issues is their being attached to new issues of *senior securities.*

In this case, Equitable Resources was selling $75,000,000 in 7-1/2% debenture bonds, the debentures due to mature in 1999. In order to facilitate the sale of the bond issue, and at an interest rate *substantially* lower than would have been the case without the Warrants added as a "sweetener," each $1,000 principal amount of bond *came with twenty Warrants.*

After issuance of the bonds, the Warrants (which is what always happens) were traded separately. Each Warrant represented the right to buy one share of common stock of Equitable Resources for $57.50 to July 1, 1992, when the Warrants would expire. This, then, was a 5-year Warrant when first issued.

Now we look at the prices for common and Warrant of Equitable Resources as we are writing, and we find the common stock selling at 40.62, and the Warrants at

NEW ISSUE   June 24, 1987

75,000 Units

Equitable Resources, Inc.

$75,000,000 Debentures, 7⅛% Series Due July 1, 1999 with
1,500,000 Common Stock Purchase Warrants

Each Unit consists of $1,000 principal amount of a Debenture and 20 five-year Warrants. The Debentures and Warrants will not be separately transferable prior to October 1, 1987 or such earlier date as may be determined by the Company with the consent of the Representative.

Each Warrant entitles the holder to purchase one share of Common Stock of the Company at a price of $57.50 per share, subject to adjustment as provided in the Prospectus, from the time the Warrants are separately transferable until July 1, 1992.

Price $1,000 Per Unit

plus accrued interest, if any, on the Debentures from the date of original issue.

Copies of the Prospectus may be obtained in any State in which this announcement is circulated only from such of the undersigned as may legally offer these securities in such State.

The First Boston Corporation

Morgan Stanley & Co.   **Shearson Lehman Brothers Inc.**   **First Manhattan Co.**
Incorporated

2.68. Our first guidepost is to divide the common price (40.62) by the Warrant price (2.68) and we have a result of *15.15*. That is a *very* high ratio number; the Warrant deserves our interest.

Our next step is to arrive at a "fair value" via our Warrant Evaluation Equation, based on the prices just given for common and Warrant.

(1) We multiply 40.62 by 1.5 and get 60.93.

(2) We multiply 60.93 by 1.5 and get 91.39.

(3) We deduct the exercise price of the Warrant (57.50) from 91.39, and get 33.89, which is the straight exercise value of the Warrant when the common is at 91.39.

(4) We take one-half of the exercise value, and get 16.95.

(5) Finally, we take one-half of the result in (4) and get *8.47*, which presumably is the fair value of the Warrant when the common is at 40.62, as it is as we write.

But the Equitable Resources Warrant is very much lower than 8.47. Indeed, it is selling at *2.68*. Does that mean that it is so greatly undervalued? Well, we *do* think it is undervalued, and in the **R.H.M. Survey** as of this writing, we have been recommending purchase of the Equitable Resources Warrant. We feel this Warrant investment will have a successful outcome, because of the favorable factors for the company, which we shall shortly describe.

But the extent of the undervaluation has to be considered in an additional frame of reference, which has to do with what kind of company Equitable Resources is, what its positive attributes are, and what those factors have to do with the anticipated action of the common stock.

The company is best known as a distributor of natural gas to customers in the Pittsburgh metropolitan area, and to parts of West Virginia and Kentucky, and its rates are subject to the rulings of the Pennsylvania Public Utility Commission. So how much common stock price excitement could there be for this company and, therefore, for the Warrant?

But in understanding *any* company, we advise the reader to *always* obtain a copy of the latest Annual Report of the company, and to study its contents with care. When we open the pages of the latest Annual Report for Equitable Resources (the 1988 Report), the picture immediately begins to expand.

In addition to the natural gas distribution business already referred to (the "Utility Service Segment"), a separate division of the company is called "The Energy Resource Segment," and is described as follows: "Energy Resources explores for, develops, produces and markets natural gas and oil in the Appalachian, Rocky Mountain and Southwest areas; performs contract drilling and well maintenance services in the Appalachian area; and extracts and markets natural gas liquids in Kentucky."

166

Here is the significant part: In 1988, while Utility Services brought in 74% of revenues, and Energy Resources only 26% of revenues, it was turned the other way around where net income was concerned. Here, Utility Services produced only 32% of net income, while Energy Resources was responsible for *68%* of net income.

Eureka! What we have here is not a staid utility, but *a natural resource company.* And further study points up the fact that Equitable Resources is rich in value where gas and oil exploration, development and production are considered.

The company's extensive acreage in the Appalachian Basin in the eastern part of the United States is the cornerstone of the Energy Resources segment of Equitable Resources. Particularly in eastern Kentucky and Virginia, natural gas in the Devonian shale is so prolific that drilling success hits the 90% rate!

Finding costs are, therefore, very low, as is lifting costs, and the gas is very rich in BTU content, increasing the value for each MCF by as much as 25%. Furthermore, since the gas finds qualify as "nonconventional gas," this production is eligible for federal income tax credits of about 75 cents per MCF of gas produced. This is equivalent to $1.14 more per MCF for gas at the wellhead.

With the above excellent picture, one need not wonder at the fact that an increase in Appalachian gas development expenditures took place from $33.4 million in 1987 to $50.6 million in 1988. This has been going on year-by-year so that each of the past seven years has seen a new record high for gas reserves. And the value of the wells discovered has been enhanced by the important fact that the productive lives of these wells are generally in excess of 30 years — an attribute which is not enjoyed by many oil and gas producers.

By December 31, 1988, proved reserves had reached 609.2 billion cubic feet of natural gas and 9.8 million barrels of oil, while 2.6 million acres are held by production, in fee and under lease, of which 1.7 million acres are undeveloped and potentially productive of natural gas and oil.

Rising energy costs are bound to increase the value of those reserves in the year ahead. The company has estimated that based on 1988 production, each 25 cent increase in the wellhead price of gas and $1.00 increase in the wellhead price of oil, adds $6 million and $800,000 respectively to net income.

And the long-term outlook is very bright for natural gas producers — particularly low-cost producers with large adjacent markets, such as enjoyed by Equitable Resources. Thus, in the **New York Times** for 11-13-88 we find: "The upward pressure on natural gas prices is expected to continue. 'Natural gas is the fuel of the future,' said Kurt H. Wulff, president of McDep Associates Inc., an oil and gas stock research firm. 'Gas has no radiation, no particulate or sulfur emissions, and generates the lowest amount of carbon dioxide of any fossil fuel.' Donald D. Dufresne, senior industry specialist for natural gas at Merrill Lynch, added, 'The demand for natural gas is exploding.' "

As we look at the price chart of the common stock

(courtesy of **Standard & Poor's**), we see the rather steady advance 1983 through 1987, temporarily interrupted in 1985, and again by the 1987 market crash. With the stock recovering to 40.62 as we write — indicated by an asterisk on the chart — the stock could well be on the way to higher levels because of the factors discussed above.

Reflecting the very large, and successful, investment of net earnings in new plant and equipment and expansion of oil and gas reserves, Net Equity per common share has advanced steadily, from $14.58 per share in 1983, to $19.21 per share in 1985 and $21.90 per share in

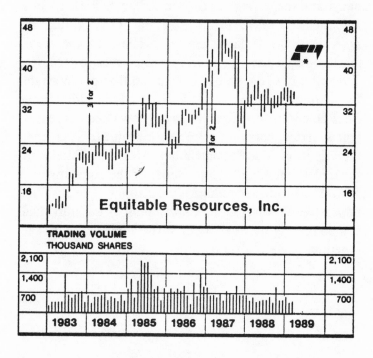

1987, while the estimate for 1989 is around the $24.50 per share level.

We have examined the picture for Equitable Resources as a company in some detail to give the reader an idea of the value of studying available information on any company in whose Warrants we develop an interest. Of particular importance is the latest Annual Report of the company in question, and a good broker usually stands ready to supply additional information from their company's research department.

In the case of Equitable Resources, it is clear that the conventional thinking in Wall Street, as we are writing, is considerably short of the mark in evaluating this company, and the *Warrants*, therefore, having a life to July 1992, clearly have profit potential. This would be *especially* true if later general declines in the stock market would push the Warrants to an even lower level.

Finally, it would be our conclusion that our Warrant Evaluation Equation is *not* very far off in judging the Equitable Resources Warrant as undervalued at the current Warrant/common price relationship. It is just that there is insufficient appreciation in financial circles of the underlying long-term potential of the company.

And one cannot emphasize too strongly, the absolute imperative to study the *fundamentals* of an individual company in order to arrive at a true appreciation of the potential of its Warrants.

Senior Securities Usable At Full Face Value In Exercising Warrants

The above heading may have a strange sound to it, but it has an important bearing on the value of quite a number of Warrants. As we have already seen, a large proportion of Warrants come into being initially attached to new issues of Bonds or Preferred Stocks — "senior securities."

The Warrants are "sweeteners" to make it easier to sell the new issue, and at terms for the senior securities that are much more advantageous for the issuing company than if there had *not* been Warrants attached.

After issuance, the senior securities and the Warrants part company, and each are thereafter traded separately. In one important sense, however, for many Warrants, a *relationship continues*, and we will describe it by picking an example — **Pan American World Airways.**

This Warrant represents the right to buy Pan Am common stock at 8.00 to May 1, 1993. In the statistical listing of this Warrant in the **R.H.M. Survey**, something is added as follows: (SS) S, 13-1/2-03, 73.00. EEP 5.84. This looks like a jumble of letters and numbers, but *it has considerable meaning*.

(SS) means there is a senior security usable at full face value in exercising the Warrant, and the "S" which follows means the senior security trades on the New York Stock Exchange. ("A" would mean the American Stock Exchange, etc.)

The name of the bond is then given as the 13-1/2s of 2003, followed by the current price of the bond, and

171

that is where the large meaning of this designation comes into play. For the best understanding of this, we go back to the first page of the original prospectus for the issuance of these Warrants, dated May 5, 1983.

It was an issue of $100,000,000 in debentures, with Warrants to purchase 10,000,000 shares of common stock, so each $1,000 principal amount of Pan Am's 13-1/2s of 2003 carried *100 Warrants*. After the issue came to market, the Warrants were "detached" and began to trade separately from the bonds.

We continue now by quoting the following from the first page of the Prospectus:

"**Warrants:** Each Warrant entitles its holder to purchase one share of Pan Am Capital Stock . . . for $8.00 . . . by tendering *cash or debentures*, which will be valued at *100% of principal amount*." (Emphasis added).

So — you can exercise the Warrants, if you wish to do so, by paying $8.00 in *cash*, or, alternately, you can tender $8.00 in principal amount (face value) of *debenture bonds* — the 13-1/2s of 2003.

The debentures will be accepted at full face value (par, or 100) in such payment, even if they are selling in the open market for *less* than 100. And in this case, the Survey information already noted tells us that with Pan Am being financially troubled, the debentures are selling on the New York Stock Exchange at *73*, as we write.

If you desired to exercise the Pan Am Warrants, it would be highly desirable to buy and tender *debenture bonds*, rather than pay the $8 per share in cash, as we now spell out.

Suppose you had 100 Warrants which you wished to exercise. You would have to pay $800 in cash plus the Warrants, to receive 100 shares of Pan Am common stock. *Instead* of that, you could buy $800 principal amount of the debenture bonds we have referred to, and since the bond is selling at *73*, it would not cost $800 to buy $800 in face value of the debentures but, rather, 73/100ths of 800, which comes to $584.

You *paid* $584 for the bonds, but you can use them as if they were $800 for purposes of exercising the Pan Am Warrants. That is why, in the Survey information, the "EEP," or Effective Exercise Price, was given as *"5.84."* With the bonds selling at 73, the effective exercise price of the Pan Am Warrant was not $8.00, but 73/100ths of $8.00, which comes to 5.84.

AMR Warrants, which we discuss next, gives us additional important insights into the price behavior of Warrants. Since AMR Warrants also have a senior security usable at full face value in exercise, we shall be reviewing the above in the context of AMR Warrants. And in the "Current Supplement" described on page 9, which is available at no cost, all Warrants which have applicable senior securities, as just described, are listed therein.

AMR Warrants

If you study a listing of the approximately 500 Warrants trading as of this writing, you will discover that they come in "all shapes and sizes"! So one should not be surprised to find that AMR Warrants (holding company for **American Airlines**) are *each* the right to buy, not *one* share of AMR common stock, but *16.19* shares. And if you exercise the Warrant, for each of those 16.19 shares you have to pay $61.766.

If we multiply 16.19 x 61.766, we get $1,000, so another way of expressing the Warrant privilege is to say that one Warrant with payment of $1,000 gets you 16.19 shares of AMR common stock.

This may seem to have been a peculiar decision of the company, along with its investment bankers, to make the Warrant privilege so complex, and even unwieldy, against the majority of Warrants, which simply say that for one Warrant you get one share of stock, at this specific price, for this period of time. But there undoubtedly was some logical reason for the decision, relating to the capital structure of the airline holding company.

In any case, there is also a *senior security* usable at full face value in exercising these AMR Warrants. When originally issued, the Warrants were attached to the American Airlines 6-1/4s of 1996, and the bond does trade on the New York Stock Exchange under the old name of American Airlines, the current price as we write being *91*. This means that instead of paying $1,000 with the Warrant for 16.19 shares of AMR, you pay 91/100ths of 1,000, or $910, through purchasing the bonds for that purpose. Of course, as the bonds fluctuate in the marketplace, you have to rework the purchase price to reflect the new prices.

Looking at the long-term price chart for AMR

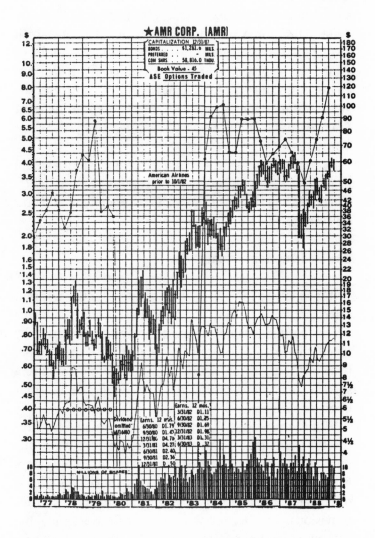

★AMR CORP. (AMR)

CAPITALIZATION 12/31/87
BONDS . . . . 61,281.0 MILS
PREFERRED . . . - MILS
COM SHRS . . . 58,816.0 THOU.
Book Value - 45
ASE Options Traded

American Airlines
prior to 10/1/82

MILLIONS OF SHARES

	Earns. 12 mos.		
Dividend		3/31/82	D1.11
omitted	Earns. 12 mos.	6/30/82	D1.25
4/16/80	6/30/80	D1.79	9/30/82 D1.69
	9/30/80	D1.43	12/31/82 D1.98
	12/31/80	D4.7b	3/31/83 D1.31
	3/31/81	D4.27i	6/30/83 D .37
	6/30/81	D2.40	
	9/30/81	D2.36	
	12/31/81	D .50	

'77 '78 '79 '80 '81 '82 '83 '84 '85 '86 '87 '88 '8

(courtesy of **Securities Research**), AMR common made a new high of 65 in 1987, and is back there again as we write. At *65* for AMR common, 16.19 shares are worth $1,052. Since, utilizing the senior security, the 16.19 shares can be purchased for $910, that gives the Warrant an exercise value of $1,052 minus $910, or *$142*. But the Warrants are selling at a premium over exercise value, at *$180*, because of the (typical) *leverage* enjoyed by the Warrant.

If, for example, AMR went to *75*, 16.19 shares would be worth $1,214, and if the bond continued to sell at 91, you could buy that package for $910, giving the Warrant an exercise value of *$304*.

The Redemption Factor

It is timely to introduce another important factor that affects quite a number of Warrants. This is a factor which *limits* the extent of the upside profit potential by specifying in the Prospectus associated with the original issue of the Warrant, that if the common moves up to a specific price, the company can *redeem* the Warrant upon payment of a stated price.

Where the AMR Warrants are concerned, the Prospectus states that if the common exceeds 115% of the then effective exercise price for at least 20 trading days within 15 days before the redemption notice date (this is the lengthy proviso typically applying to most "Call" provisions, whether for Warrants, or Convertibles), the Warrants can be redeemed by AMR upon payment by the company of $43.75 through February 1990, $37.50

through February 1991, and lower prices thereafter.

Since the exercise price is actually $1,000 for 16.19 shares, if AMR common reached a price level where the exercise value was *$1,150*, the right of AMR to redeem would go into effect. This point would be reached with AMR common at about *71*, for 16.19 shares at 71 are worth about $1,150, which would be 115% of the exercise price.

Here, the right to use the senior security at full face value would be *very* useful, because with the package of stock worth $1,150, the right to buy that package for *$910* (the American Airlines bond at 91) would give the Warrant a value of 1,150 minus 910, or *240*. If the redemption Call was announced, therefore, the holder of the Warrant could *exercise* the Warrant, receive the 16.19 shares of AMR and avoid the redemption at $43.75.

Of course, at lower levels for AMR, the Warrants did not have to concern themselves with redemption, and one could concentrate on the *leverage potential*. In late-1987, AMR common had dropped to the 27 level and the AMR Warrant was selling at *35*. In the subsequent advance, the common stock went fom 27 to 65, up *140%*, while the *Warrants* had a much greater move, from 35 to *180*, up *414%*.

Should AMR common stock decline in any subsequent bear market, the Warrants would again have its leverage potential, and this must be kept in mind.

In analyzing the value of *any* Warrant, it should be clear from the foregoing that one must be alert to (a) the possible right to use a senior security at full face value in exercising the Warrant — this can make a *large* difference — and (b) any *redemption* clauses affecting the Warrant privilege.

Warrants — A Two-Way Street!

The way we have approched "Opportunities in Warrants" in the past 37 years has been two-pronged. First, many new Warrants that come on the scene as a result of mergers or acquisitions, where stockholders of the company being acquired receive *Warrants* as part of their buyout "package," are almost automatically a "Buy."

This is because the former stockholders receiving those Warrants are almost universally unfamiliar with what Warrants *are*, and having already typically received a well-above-market-price for their stock, are quite willing to regard the Warrants that came along in tow as "icing on the cake," to be sold for whatever they will bring.

Thus, we have seen spelled out the bargain aspects of the **Eli Lilly Warrant,** the **General Tire & Rubber Warrants** and the **Capital Cities/ABC Warrants,** and new Warrants along the same lines come on the scene in an unceasing flow. At times the flow quickens, other times it slows, but the advent of new Warrants, on many levels, never stops.

Secondly, and more numerous, are Warrants that have been driven down to lower prices, often *much* lower prices, as the individual company, and/or the stock market itself, have gotten into trouble. The sequence of "getting into trouble," and then "getting out of trouble" has been productive of many large-scale profits with Warrants, as very low-price, even "pennies" Warrants, turn around with their common stocks and race up to the "dollars" level.

Waiting for these lower Warrant prices to develop, which is the usual course of action we recommend, implies that speculators who buy *high*-price Warrants very often end up as big losers.

That "implication" is exactly correct, and we demonstrate it by setting forth some disasters that occurred with a number of Warrant issues in recent years. What we recount is also instructive as to additional avenues by which Warrants come into existence, as well as other important factors.

American Telephone & Telegraph Warrants

We begin by interjecting a comment that we are *not* referring to A T & T *Scores*, which are also Warrants, but quite different than the Warrants we now describe. In later pages we will be discussing the *very promising* A T & T *Scores*.

In 1970, a giant Warrant issue came into being, created by another giant — **American Telephone & Telegraph**. Desirous of raising some additional capital, A T & T announced a "rights" offering, by which the existing stockholders got the first crack at purchasing an issue of bonds with Warrants attached.

The holders of each 35 shares of common stock of A T & T would be entitled to subscribe to $100 in debenture bonds *plus 2 Warrants*. Since there were fully

549,263,000 shares of A T & T outstanding in 1970 (!), this worked out to 15,693,000 Units, which would result in *31,386,400 Warrants* to be outstanding. Meanwhile A T & T would raise $3.1 billion on the offering of bonds with Warrants, and if the Warrants were eventually *exercised*, another $1.72 billion would come into the till.

We now see clearly, with this example, what corporations are after when they issue bonds with Warrants attached. Firstly, the addition of the Warrants as "sweeteners," *always* results in a sizable saving in the "coupon" of the bond portion. That is, the issue with Warrants enables the company to market the issue with a much lower interest rate than would be true if it were a "straight" bond without any Warrants.

Secondly, should the Warrants be *exercised* within its span of allotted time, an additional influx of capital would come in at a considerably higher price for the common than was typically true when the issue was originally marketed. A new issue of "bonds with Warrants" makes a great deal of sense!

The issue was duly sold, and the exercise privilege of the Warrant was the right to buy one share of A T & T common stock at 52.00 to May 15, 1975, when the Warrants would expire. The new Warrants promptly sold up to *13.00*, with the common stock at 51-5/8.

If we divide the common price by the Warrant price (51.62 by 13), which is always our first quick test of whether a Warrant holds interest, we get 3.97, which is a "passable" ratio, and when we apply our Warrant Evaluation Equation, as previously described, we find that a "fair value" for the new A T & T Warrant was *16*, not much more than the 13 Warrant price.

Here we have an opportunity to emphasize a point which we started to analyze with the **Equitable Resources Warrant**, where the "fair value" price for the Warrant was far higher than the Warrant price, but explainable in part because the company — Equitable Resources — was regarded by the financial community as a "public utility," the common stock having limited upside potential.

In the case of Equitable Resources, we explained that the company was actually an undervalued *natural resource entity*, so that the Warrant had much more value than seemed immediately apparent. But in the case of **A T & T**, it fell completely into the category of "public utility," all its rates then regulated by public authorities, a lid established on its profits, along with other inhibitions, making highly unlikely any multiplication of the market price for its common stock over the near term.

As a consequence, we did not recommend purchase of this new issue of A T & T Warrants, feeling it was fully priced at 13, and in view of what subsequently happened with those Warrants, we are quite pleased with our then decision.

Looking at the price action of A T & T common stock from 1970 through 1975 (chart courtesy of **Securities Research**), we have drawn a line through the price action at *52*, which was then the exercise price of the A T & T Warrant, and it is to be noted that the common stock hardly ever did more than "peek" through that line during the 1970-1975 period, and then sold down to the 40s as the Warrant approached the May 1975 expiration date, with the result that the Warrant *expired worthless.*

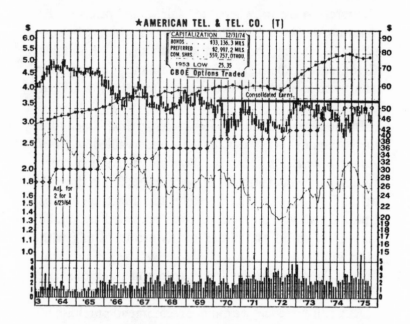

Now, at its 13 top, the 31,386,400 A T & T Warrants had a market value of about *$408 million*, which totally vanished when the Warrants expired at 0 value. Warrants are most distinctly a "two-way" street!

American Express/Fireman's Fund Warrants

Up to October 1985, Fireman's Fund, an insurance company prominent in property and casualty insurance, had been a wholly-owned subsidiary of American Express since 1968, until 32.5 million common shares were sold at $25.75 per share, 27.2 million shares being sold for American Express, and the balance for Fireman's Fund. The stock having had a run to the upside in early 1986, reaching the 44-1/2 level, American Express decided to sell off more of its holdings.

American Express has had a history of understanding the uses of Warrants, and in May 1986 came up with a proposed sale of 6,400,000 Units, each Unit to consist of one share of Fireman's Fund, and one Warrant to buy *1/2* share of Fireman's Fund at a price of $43.70 until March 31, 1989, when the Warrants would expire.

The knowledgeable American Express management added *Warrants* as a sweetener, which caused the issue to be a sellout, and American Express saw *$256,960,000 flow into its coffers*, net of the underwriting discount and commissions.

It is important to emphasize that *it was not* Fireman's Fund that was selling the issue, but American Express, and the Warrants could be exercised for Fireman's Fund common stock that was owned by American Express. There are quite a number of occasions when a company that owns a substantial number of shares of another company will issue Warrants *on* those shares. For example, on previous pages we described how **Cities Service** issued a large bond issue carrying Warrants for **Atlantic Richfield** shares owned by Cities Service.

A few months after the sale of the common/Warrants issue, there was a modest advance in Fireman's Fund common stock, and in August of that year, the common stock was at 37.87 and the Warrants were selling at *5* on the American Stock Exchange. Since it took *two* Warrants to buy one share of common, the actual prices were 37.87 for the common and *10.00* for *two* Warrants, representing the right to buy one share of common stock at $43.70, as already discussed.

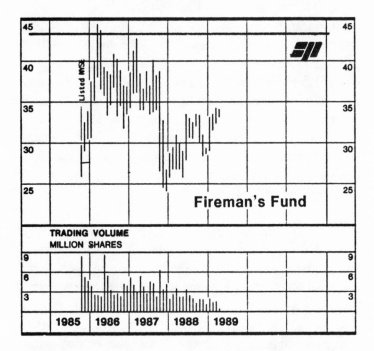

The chart (courtesy of **Standard & Poor's**) tells us that Fireman's Fund traversed a sideways path, 1966 through 1987, until the October 1987 market crash. In any case, we have drawn a line through the exercise price of the Warrant (43.70), and just as with A T & T, the common stock never did get through that line, which event would have begun to develop intrinsic value for the Warrants.

184

The Warrant was always traded on the American Stock Exchange as the *American Express* Warrant, and it was never an attractive Warrant. Thus, taking the prices of 37.87 for the common and 10.00 for two Warrants, if the common had moved up 50% from 37.875 to 56.80, that would have given the Warrants an intrinsic value of 56.80 minus 43.70, or 13.10.

Even allowing for a premium above intrinsic value, it is still difficult to see how the Warrants could have exceeded the percentage move in the common stock. On the other hand, the Warrants could be expected to *decline* at a faster rate than the common stock, if that was the direction the common stock would take. Clearly, the Warrant could not be considered for purchase.

1989 came with Fireman's Fund common stock quite a distance from the exercise level, and the Warrants expired at 0 — worthless. With some other sales of the same Warrant, the final total outstanding was 8 million Warrants, and at the 5 level, where it started trading, this had been worth *$40 million.*

By March 31, 1989, the entire $40 million had disappeared without a trace!

We trust we have made it clear that each Warrant must be analyzed with care, to avoid those that have little or no promise, and to seize opportunities which have *large* promise. That is why we have presented such contrasting pictures as that for, say, **Eli Lilly Warrants** and **Fireman's Fund Warrants.** Each Warrant is very much a separate entity, and must be analyzed as such.

A Series of Warrant Studies
Contributes Valuable Insights

There now follow discussions of a number of individual Warrants, *each* of which sheds light on a number of important aspects of Warrant analysis and understanding.

Sallie Mae Warrants

In July 1986, the Student Loan Marketing Association (Sallie Mae) sold 300,000 Units, bringing in net proceeds of $296,940,000 to the company, and "blazing a trail" in that two different *Warrants* were part of the offering, including *Put* Warrants.

That is, each Unit consisted of $1,000 principal amount of a 5.60% Note, 12 *Call Warrants* and 6 *Put Warrants*. Each Call Warrant represented the right to buy one share of Sallie Mae, which traded on the New York Stock Exchange, for $100, until August 1, 1991, when the Warrant would expire.

Each Put Warrant, to quote the Prospectus: " . . . entitles the holder to tender to Sallie Mae one share of Nonvoting Common Stock for mandatory purchase by Sallie Mae at a price of $51 . . . until August 1, 1991."

So, if Sallie Mae common would subsequently decline in the marketplace to, say, *30*, the Put would be worth a minimum of 51 minus 30, or *21*. For just as we previously explained about the role of the professional arbitrageur, ever alert for such opportunities, if the Put would sell for *less* than 21, with Sallie Mae common at

30, the arbitrageur could buy the Put, and one share of Sallie Mae common in the open market, and sell the combination to the company for $51.

Sallie Mae had its origin as part of President Lyndon Johnson's "Great Society" program, and aimed squarely at "doing good" for the middle class — a very large block of voters! In the "Guaranteed Student Loan Program," loans would be made to college student applicants by private lenders, mostly banks, with the interest rate subsidized in substantial part by the government and *both principal and interest for these loans to be guaranteed by the federal government.*

Like any other federal guarantee, this ensured enthusiastic lenders. A steadily growing number of college students rushed to take advantage of loans whose interest rate was about 3-1/2% under the then going rate, and with no repayment due until after graduation. The growth in the program is illustrated by the chart shown (courtesy of the **New York Times**), taken from a study-in-depth we did for this new Warrant in the **R.H.M. Survey** of August 15, 1986, following our "Buy" recommendation for the "Call" Warrant a few weeks earlier.

The Student Loan Marketing Association came into being in 1972 as a result of Congress amending the Higher Education Act of 1965. Since student loans under the Guaranteed Student Loan Program were growing so fast, a need was becoming more insistent to provide increased liquidity to the various entities that were making loans to students. These loans were still being made mostly by banks, but also involved were educational institutions and state agencies.

The Student Loan Marketing Association (Sallie Mae) would create a secondary market for all of these

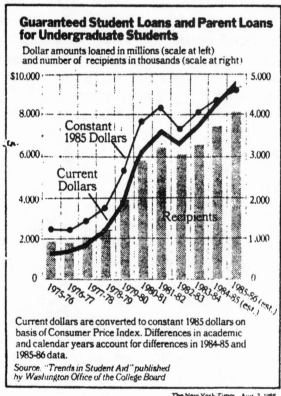

Guaranteed Student Loans and Parent Loans for Undergraduate Students

Dollar amounts loaned in millions (scale at left) and number of recipients in thousands (scale at right)

Current dollars are converted to constant 1985 dollars on basis of Consumer Price Index. Differences in academic and calendar years account for differences in 1984-85 and 1985-86 data.

Source: "Trends in Student Aid" published by Washington Office of the College Board

The New York Times, Aug 3, 1986

188

loans, enabling the original lending institutions to sell their loans to Sallie Mae when they needed to free their money. Sallie Mae would also enter into commitment contracts to buy these loans over a specified time in the future, increasing flexibility for lending institutions.

With all of the student loans ultimately guaranteed by the U.S. Government, the fees earned by Sallie Mae were free of risk, and the continuing growth of the Guaranteed Student Loan Program ensured that Sallie Mae's earnings were going to grow and grow.

When we first recommended purchase of the Warrants, the prices were 53-1/4 for the common stock and 4-5/8 for the Warrant. With the exercise price (100) so far distant from the then price of the common stock, the "fair price" for the Warrant, using our "Warrant Evaluation" formula, worked out to just about what the Warrant was selling for — 4-5/8.

But another measure, dividing the common stock price by the Warrant price, was very favorable to the Warrant — 53.25 divided by 4.625 equaled *11.51*. Another favorable factor was our expectation that the common stock would rise, propelled by what we deemed to be an inevitable increase in earnings.

And this indeed is what happened, well illustrated by the price chart for the common stock (courtesy of **Securities Research**). Note the climbing earnings, shown by the dot-connected line giving earnings quarter-by-quarter.

Having recommended purchase when selling at 4-5/8 in the August 1, 1986 Survey, we recommended taking profits in the February 20, 1987 Survey, a bit more

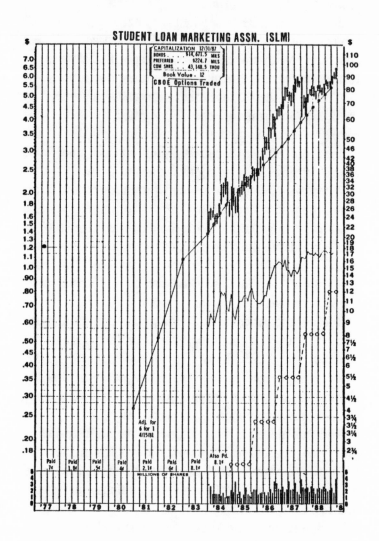

190

than six months later, when selling at 15.00. Our feeling about Warrant profits in such situations is that if you have already enjoyed a *substantial* gain, and the remaining dynamism in the common stock has to have lessened to at least some extent, it is usually better to take the profit, and leave any remaining run in the Warrants to someone more speculatively-minded.

After all, there is a *very* significant difference between a Warrant selling at 4-5/8 and one selling at *15*. At the 4-5/8 mark, any decline in the Warrant would induce stronger and stronger resistance to further decline, because potential *leverage* would increase sharply at those lower price levels. But at *15*, there is nothing to prevent the Warrant from running back towards that 4-5/8 price, if the common stock begins to slip in the marketplace.

Where the *Put* Options are concerned, they started out around the 6 level and stand at 25 cents as we are writing. We have never recommended the Puts for purchase, but should a substantial market slide look to us to be in the offing, we would certainly *consider* making a "Buy" recommendation, because of the very low price, and the possibility that Congress and the Administration might seek to rein in the student loan program because of the shockingly high rate of default in the program.

When the individuals who took the loans cease to repay principal, along with required interest, the *lenders* do not suffer, for they are paid in full by the government, or should we say, the taxpayers!

The Sallie Mae Put Option deserves watching for a later opportunity. The major lesson to be learned with the Sallie Mae Warrant is that when the common stock is such a high multiple of the Warrant price (11.51, remember), and the common stock has good potential for advancing, via earnings growth for the company, the Warrant is almost surely worth purchase.

Companies Selling "Naked" Warrants

Thus far we have seen companies raising capital by selling Warrants attached to new Bond issues and to issues of common stock, but **Intel Corp.** went in quite another direction by selling Warrants attached to nothing! This is why we call them "naked."

Note on the excerpts shown from two different Prospectuses, both involving the sale of "naked" Warrants, that the *first* sale took place on March 25, 1987, when 3,500,000 Warrants were sold at a price of $10 each, and after allowances for "Underwriting Discount and Commissions," Intel received a net $33,250,000 on the sale.

This felt so good, and made so much sense, that less than four months later, Intel was doing the same thing again, except that this time they sold *6,000,000* Warrants at $10 each, bringing in a net $57,480,000.

Something else happened with the last-named Warrant issue, which was the right to buy at $45 per share to *August 15, 1988.* It was only a *one-year Warrant,* and the ability of the company to sell a Warrant issue of such short duration illustrates the *appetite* of investors for Warrants — a point we shall have more to say about.

PROSPECTUS
March 25, 1987

CORPORATION

Warrants to Purchase
3,500,000 Shares
of Capital Stock

PROSPECTUS
August 7, 1987

CORPORATION

Warrants to Purchase
6,000,000 Shares
of Capital Stock

Adjusting Warrant Exercise Terms
For Stock Splits

In September 1987, Intel split its common stock 3-for-2. This meant that every 200 shares became 300 shares, and the Warrant terms were adjusted for that event. The Warrant that had been sold in March 25, 1987 became the right to buy *1.5* shares at *$30* per share, whereas it had previously been the right to buy 1 share for $45.00.

And a 10-year Warrant which had originally been sold in May 1985 became the right to buy *1.5* shares at *26.67* per share to May 15, 1995. The right to have Warrant terms adjusted for stock splits or, in many cases, even for smaller stock dividends, is very important to maintaining the value of a Warrant.

Some Additional Significant Points

The one-year Warrant that Intel had sold in August 1987, reached the end of its life in August 1988 as the right to buy 1.5 shares for each Warrant, at $30 per share. Or, to put it another way, each Warrant could buy 1.5 shares for $45.

Now, in early-August 1988, Intel was selling at $35, so 1.5 shares were worth *$52.50*. The right to buy a package worth $52.50 for $45 is worth $7.50, which meant that anyone holding the Warrants *rushed to exercise them* prior to the expiration date of 8-15-88, because if they did not do so, they lost the difference between $52.50 and $45.00.

Intel Corp. was able to announce as follows: "August 16, 1988: Company announced that it had received approximately $268,600,000 from the exercise of Warrants that expired on August 15. Company stated that the Warrants, each of which had entitled holders thereof to purchase capital shares at $30 per share, had been exercised for approximately 8,900,000 capital shares."

This meant that not only had Intel received a net $57,480,000 when it had *sold* 6,000,000 Warrants at $10 per Warrant in August 1987, but when the Warrants were *exercised*, because the common stock price was above the exercise price at expiration date, another $268,600,000 came into the company's treasury.

This totaled *$326,080,000* for a *one-year Warrant*, and raises the question: why do not *more* companies sell "naked" Warrants, when they can easily raise substantial amounts of new capital in this manner, in a very advantageous way? What we have described for Intel is a very flexible means of raising capital.

Thus, a Warrant can be, say, of 3 years duration, or 5 years, or even 10 years, and the exercise price can be set well above the price of the stock upon issuance. This guarantees that if the Warrants are ever exercised, the price of the common stock will have moved considerably higher, so, in effect, stock will have been sold at a high price, which should make all the stockholders happy (and the company's finance officer too!)

Another way of looking at this is as follows: If the Warrant has a lengthy duration, and the exercise price has been set well above the common price upon issuance, it is certain that the Warrant will never be exercised until expiration date comes close. For the extended life of the Warrant will almost always cause a *premium above exercise value* to be paid for the Warrant. So even if the common subsequently moves up close to the exercise price, the premium over exercise value will prevent immediate exercise, since in doing so, the then current size of a premium would represent a *loss*! So no one will be foolish enough to exercise such a Warrant.

And what does this mean for the corporation that issued the Warrant? It means the corporation can utilize the large sums received when the Warrants were originally sold *for a long time*, before the possibility of exercise becomes a factor. We feel it to be logical that before too long, more companies will get the message as we have just described it, and will be selling issues of "naked," or "stand alone" Warrants, which will add to the hundreds of Warrants already trading today.

The Two Intel Warrants

Meanwhile, what about the two remaining Intel Warrants that have some years to run? We feel that they will become excellent trading mediums over the next year or so as the general market goes into some wide market swings to reflect an economy poised on the verge of recession.

Intel, of course, has an outstanding reputation in designing and manufacturing semiconductor components and microcomputer systems, as well as computer software for original equipment manufacturers. The company was the first in the field to introduce a microprocessor, and this goes all the way back to 1971. Today it is preeminent in "erasable, programmable, read-only memories," — EPROMS for short.

Earnings have reflected the ups and downs of the semiconductor industry, which also shows up in the price chart for the company (courtesy of **Standard &**

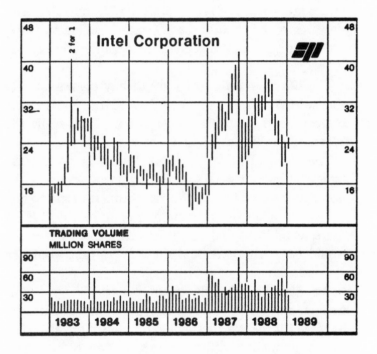

Poor's). This leads us to believe that with a later *downswing* for the stock market, both the common stock and the two Warrants could get down to levels where opportunity would "knock" — particularly for the Warrants, which would have considerable leverage if the price gets low enough.

As we write, the common stock is at 31-7/8, and the **'95 Warrant**, being the right to buy 1.5 shares at 26.67 per share to 5-15-95, is selling at 14.81. Buying 1.5 shares at 26.67 per share comes to paying $40.00 for those shares, and if we consider that at 31-7/8, 1.5 shares are worth 47.81, that gives the Warrant an intrinsic value of *7.81*. Since the Warrant is selling at *14.81*, that represents a substantial premium over exercise value.

The **'92 Warrant** is the right to buy those same 1.5 shares at 30.00 per share to 3-15-92 (or $45 for 1.5 shares), so the intrinsic value is only *2.81*, while the Warrant is selling at *11.68* as we write.

The elevated prices for both Warrants reflects the esteem in which Intel is held by investors, and the leverage involved in each Warrant being the right to buy *1.5* shares. Thus, if the common ran up to, say, *50*, 1.5 shares would be worth *75.00*, and then the '92 Warrant would be worth *30.00* and the '95 Warrant would be worth *35.00*.

We feel the *other* direction is more likely, at this writing, and depending on the depth of any decline, the leverage for the Warrants could become impressive. The foregoing has served the purpose not only of analyzing the potential of **Intel's** two Warrants, but of giving the reader some idea of how many varieties of opportunities there can be in a list of *500* different Warrants!

This would be particularly true if the general market entered a period of *wide swings*, periods of sharp decline, followed by periods of equally sharp recoveries. And this, indeed, is what we expect to happen.

"A" and "B" Warrants

In recent years, a goodly number of Warrant issues, particularly for more speculative situations, have not been content with offering *one* Warrant, but included a provision that when a Warrant is exercised, another Warrant is received, typically called a "B" Warrant. This provision can have a considerable effect on the valuation of a Warrant, and an example now follows.

Management Company Entertainment Group Warrants

In August 1987, this company sold 800 Units, each Unit consisting of 10,000 shares of common stock, and 10,000 Class A Warrants, the Unit costing $10,000. Each Class A Warrant was the right for five years to buy one share of common stock for $1.50, but *with* the exercise of the Warrant for that one share of stock, one would also receive a Class "B" Warrant. The Class B Warrant, in turn, would be the right, for five years, to buy a share of common stock for $2.25.

As another typical provision for these more speculative Warrants, the Company had the right to redeem both Warrants at a price of five cents per Warrant on 15 days notice, *providing*, however, that the common stock sold in excess of $2.10 per share for the "A" Warrant, and $3.15 per share for the "B" Warrant, for a period of 15 consecutive business days.

Management Co. Entertainment Group planned to operate in the areas of motion picture production and distribution, and in "talent management." Having connections with a large number of foreign subdistributors in more than 150 countries, as the company has stated, the potential in distributing low-budget, and medium-budget films was thought to be considerable. As of the fiscal year ended 3-31-88, earnings were only $0.03 per share, while "Book Value" was stated as $0.36 per share.

When it comes to "entertainment" companies, however, speculative interest can ride high, and the price chart (courtesy of Long Term Values) does indeed show a steady rise in the common stock since a late-1987 low. Indeed, as we write, the common stock has reached *3-7/8*, while the "A" Warrants are selling at *4.00* and the "B" Warrants at *1.81*.

Why would the "A" Warrant be selling at a higher price than the common stock? This is understandable because of the "B" Warrant which would be received upon exercise.

Thus, the "A" Warrant is the right to buy at *1.50*, so with the common at 3.87, there is intrinsic value of *2.37*. With the "B" Warrant selling at 1.81, that increases the intrinsic value of the "A" Warrant to 2.37 plus 1.81, or *4.18*

Even if Management Company Entertainment Group would decide to redeem the "A" Warrants (the stock is selling above the required 2.10 level, and enough time has passed above that price), the Warrant holders have 15 days to exercise their Warrants, receiving one share of common stock and one "B" Warrant. So announcement of a redemption does not mean you have to sell your Warrant for five cents!

201

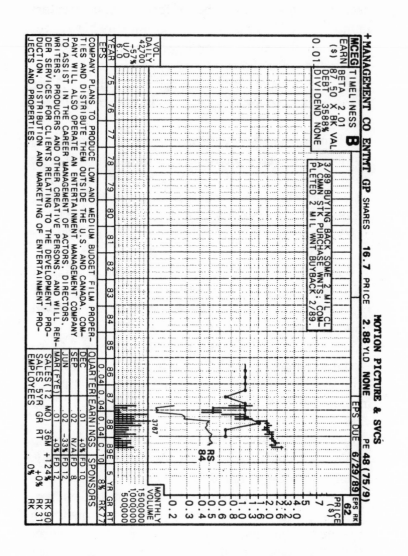

This points up the need to respect the dozens of speculative, low-price Warrants that have the same type of provisions that we have just described, with "A" and "B" and sometimes "C" Warrants in the picture! If such Warrants are available at very low prices during periods of sharp market decline, they could well represent speculative opportunities *if* growth potential can be seen for the company that issued the Warrants, and *if* the financial situation of the company is such that survivability is not in question.

Warrant Opportunities Ahead On Many Levels

As we are writing, the period of economic expansion in this country is in its *seventh year*, while, at the same time, an insupportable level of debt is piling up in many sectors of the economy.

This means that when recession comes on the scene (this is inevitable, and not far removed in point of time), it will become a *dangerous* recession, and will deepen quickly, because many sectors of business and individuals can hardly manage their debt load while the economy is still *expanding*, which translates into a stream of domino-type bankruptcies when the economy turns down.

We feel that these dangers are fully recognized by the Federal Reserve Board, the Administration and Congress, and that at a certain point in the downturn, the floodgates of credit will be thrown open wide in an all-out effort to jolt the economy back into a growth pattern, along with prodigious "bailout" moves from Washington.

When recession takes hold, corporate earnings will be hit hard on an almost immediate basis, and along with gathering distress from the debt-laden, the stock market will experience a very substantial decline. But when inflation-producing governmental action comes into play to turn the economy around, we feel there is every chance that *a new bull market* will then begin.

A down-then-up stock market is *made-to-order* for leveraged opportunities with hundreds of long-term

Warrants on many levels, from moderate leverage to high leverage, and at this point we analyze two categories of Warrant action, by two different examples, which provide good understanding of the multiplicity of Warrant opportunities that are directly ahead.

Hotel Properties Warrants

Hotel Properties Inc. owned extensive real estate interests in California and other western states, and did well on the American Stock Exchange, 1984 - 1986, the common stock rising from 11-5/8 to 20-7/8, *up 80%*.

There were *Warrants* outstanding for Hotel Properties, each Warrant representing the right to buy one share of common at *13.00 to 4-30-89*. When the common was selling at 11-5/8, the Warrant — the right to buy at *13* — was selling at 1-3/8 but had no immediate exercise value. The 1-3/8 being paid for the Warrants simply measured their speculative potential in the event that the common stock moved *above* the 13 level, where exercise value would begin to build.

When the common did advance to *20-7/8*, the Warrant, being the right to buy at 13.00, had a minimum exercise value of 20-7/8 minus 13, or 7-7/8, and actually sold at *8.00*. Some simple arithmetic throws a bright searchlight on the *leverage potential* of "ordinary" Warrant opportunities, when we go over the above figures once again.

In exactly the same 1984 - 1986 period:

Hotel Properties *common* had moved
from 11-7/8 to 20-7/8 . . . . . up 80 %

While Hotel Properties *Warrants* had
moved from 1-3/8 to 8 . . . . . up 482 %

The Hotel Properties Warrants had advanced
6 times faster than Hotel Properties
common stock on the upside.

Again illustrating the crucial point that Warrants can so often be a *far* better buy than their respective common stock, consider this factor: If Hotel Properties common, instead of advancing, had *declined* by 50%, from 11-5/8 to about 5-7/8, the *Warrant* could also have declined by 50% from 1-3/8 to 68 cents, without showing any greater percentage decline than the common stock.

Yet, our decades of experience in following many hundreds of Warrants on a daily basis, tells us that with the common at 5-7/8, and the Warrant still having some years to run — the expiration date was April 1989 — it was *highly unlikely* that the Warrant would have sold below 68 cents.

At the prices then, of 11-5/8 for Hotel Properties common and 1-3/8 for the Hotels Properties Warrants, we had a situation where the Warrants did advance 6 times faster than the common stock on the *up*side, but promised to do no worse on a percentage basis than the common stock on the *down*side. The Warrant had been a greatly superior "Buy" as against the common stock.

What we have just described, and there were many similar examples in earlier pages, will be true of *hundreds* of common/Warrant price relationships in the months ahead, which have high potential for rewarding the reader's close attention.

GEICO Warrants

One could begin describing the high-leverage opportunity that developed for GEICO Warrants by asking the question: How could a *$500* investment in one common stock Warrant become worth *$608,000* in a few years?

And there is an answer to that question that will be meaningful for *hundreds* of Warrant opportunities when the next large downturn for the stock market comes on the scene.

That answer is: The company that issued the Warrants got *into* trouble, and then got *out* of trouble. This, of course, is exactly what will happen in many instances when, first, *recession* hits, along with a falling stock market, which will cause *many* companies to get *into* trouble.

This will be followed by all-out Federal Reserve Board and Washington action, which will get many of those companies *out* of trouble and very probably *also* get the stock market "out of trouble." What is coming, then, is a "down-then-up" stock market, which is always the best setting for high-leverage Warrant events.

A close look at how the GEICO Warrant situation developed will be highly instructive for these later Warrant opportunities to come. The GEICO Corporation is a successor to the Government Employees Insurance Corp., and we begin by quoting **Fortune** for 9-5-83, which had a major article headlined "Muddling To Victory at GEICO," with the opening sentence stating: "When Byrne took charge of the Washington D.C. auto insurer in 1976, it was on the verge of bankruptcy . . . "

That same note was struck by another article on GEICO in **Business Week** (9-12-83) which began: "GEICO Corp, on the brink of collapse in 1976 . . . "

If you want to see GEICO's common stock collapsing, look at the chart on the next page (courtesy of **Securities Research**), and note the toboggan slide from 60 in 1972 to about *3-1/8* in 1976, with the company having suffered heavy losses in 1975 and 1976 — a loss of ($7.00) per share in 1975 alone.

A reorganization, during which existing Warrants got an extension of life to 1983, put the company on the road to recovery under the leadership of Chairman John J. Byrne, and earnings got back on the upswing trail.

Dividend payments were reinstated during that period, and climbed year-by-year, and the result for the *common stock* is shown on the chart by a V-like recovery, so that during 1983, GEICO common stock actually returned to its old high at *60.*

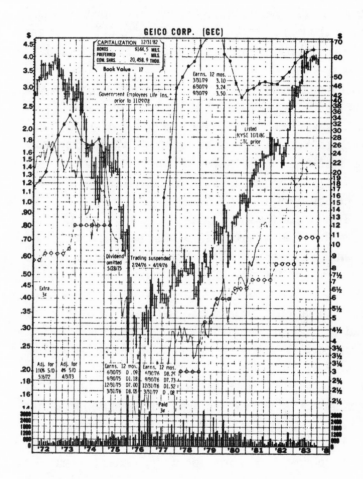

GEICO CORP. (GEC)

The major reason that the greatest profit opportunities in Warrants come when the company that issued the Warrants gets into trouble, is that the pessimism engendered by the sinking of the common stock, and often the real threat of bankruptcy, causes the Warrant to fall to very low prices, very often to the "pennies" level.

If the company is then able to get *out* of trouble and get back to profitability, a rising stock market will very often take the common stock to a high level of recovery, and the Warrant then suddenly has a *large* market value because of its right to be exchanged for that common stock, at a specific price for a specific period of time. (The definition of a Warrant!)

This is exactly what happened to the GEICO Warrant. In 1978, when GEICO was in a very weakened position, the records of the National Quotation Bureau show a low for the GEICO Warrant of 1/16 (6-1/4 cents), which rebounded to 1-5/8 in 1979 as the reorganization took hold and the threat of bankruptcy faded.

As earnings and the common stock climbed, the *Warrant* advanced. Finally, in 1983, with each Warrant representing the right to buy 2.08 shares of GEICO common at $24 per share, when the common stock hit its high of *60* that year, the right to buy *one* share at 24 had a minimum worth of 60 minus 24 or 36, and the right to buy *2.08* shares for each Warrant meant the Warrant had a minimum value of 2.08 times 36, or $74.88, with the actual recorded high for the Warrant being *$76.00.*

The leverage here proved to be literally enormous.

Thus, if anyone was so fortunate as to have put $500 into 8,000 GEICO Warrants at the 6-1/4 cents low, by the time the Warrant hit $76, as it *had* to once the common stock reached 60, that **$500** speculation had become worth **$608,000**.

Even a mere **$62.50** in 1,000 Warrants became worth **$76,000** in that same period of time.

This, then, is the kind of remarkable profit potential which develops with a long-term Warrant when there is the process of the company that issued the Warrants first getting *into* trouble, and then getting *out* of trouble.

It emphasizes the fact that the reader should be carefully watching a host of developing Warrant opportunities over the next year or two, while the country *as a whole* gets *into* trouble, and then gets *out* of trouble. Opportunities, among the hundreds of Warrants trading today, with new Warrants coming on the scene in a regular flow, will range from the moderate, but still very rewarding, leverage such as we described with **Hotel Properties Warrants**, and the extremely high leverage we have just described with **GEICO Warrants**.

We expect Warrant opportunities over the next year or two to be of an *historic* nature.

American Stock Exchange

52-Weeks High	52-Weeks Low	Name and Dividend	Sales 100s	Yield Pct.	P/E Ratio	Week's High	Week's Low	Last	Net Chg.
38⅞	38¾	A-axp un							
27¼	25⅜	A-axp pr	381	...	...	26½	25½	26	− ½
14	7½	A-axp sc	1880	...	...	14	12⅝	13½	.....
91	79¼	A-ahp un3.29							
70	63⅝	A-ahp pr3.29	349	4.7	...	70	69	69½	...
26	10½	A-ahp sc	436	...	...	u26	23½	23½	− 2
33⅜	23¼	A-att2 un1.15							
23⅝	18¾	A-att2 pr1.15	115	5.0	...	23⅜	22⅝	22⅞	− ½
14⅞	4	A-att2 sc	4566	...	...	14¼	12½	13⅝	− ½
90	84¼	A-an un3.25							
68½	55	A-an pr 3.25	89	4.9	...	66¾	63½	66¾	+ 2½
30¼	15¾	A-an sc	512	...	...	16⅞	d15¾	16	− ¾
98¼	93⅝	A-arc un3.95							
78⅛	72	A-arc pr3.95	41	5.4	...	75	d72	73¼	− 2¼
23¼	18½	A-arc sc	245	...	...	21⅛	18½	20¼	− ½
110	94	A-bmy un2.75	10	2.7	...	106	102	103½	− 3½
75½	66	A-bmy pr2.75	5	3.8	...	73	72	72	− 2
36¾	25¼	A-bmy sc	179	...	...	33¼	30¾	32½	− ¼
61¾	60¼	A-chv un2.35							
52	45	A-chv pr2.35	15	5.1	...	46½	46	46½	− ¾
14¾	11½	A-chv sc	637	...	...	14⅜	12⅛	14¼	+ 1¾
55½	47⅞	A-ko un 1.07	41	1.9	...	u55½	52½	55½	+ 2
34	31	A-ko pr 1.07	89	3.3	...	33¾	32⅝	32¾	− ¾
24⅜	11½	A-ko sc	2695	...	...	u24⅜	20¼	24⅜	+ 4½
86½	80¼	A-dow un2.15							
72	56½	A-dow pr2.15	3	3.1	...	71	70⅜	70⅜	− ⅝
31	19¼	A-dow sc	590	...	...	u31	25½	30¾	+ 3½
128⅝	100½	A-dd un3.35							
80½	71	A-dd pr 3.35	15	4.2	...	80	80	80	− ½
49⅜	21⅛	A-dd sc	100	...	...	u49⅜	45½	49¼	+ 1
97½	66½	A-xon un3.95	1	4.1	...	u97½	97½	97½	+ 1
60½	52⅝	A-xon pr3.95	114	6.6	...	59¾	59¼	59¾	+ ½
40½	10¾	A-xon sc	1026	...	...	39⅝	36¼	39⅝	+ 2⅛
45⅜	38¼	A-gte un2.47							
34	31⅛	A-gte pr 2.47	x1846	7.7	...	33⅝	31¼	32⅛	− ⅝
13	6¾	A-gte sc	3738	...	...	12⅞	11¼	12⅜	.....
125	106⅛	A-ge un 2.59	20	2.1	...	125	124	124	− 1
89	72½	A-ge pr 2.59	126	3.0	...	87½	86½	87½	− ½
46¼	24	A-ge sc	421	...	...	u46¼	38⅞	45¾	+ 5¾
88	84	A-gm un4.95							
71¾	69	A-gm pr4.95	615	7.1	...	70	69¼	69⅜	− ⅜
26	10¾	A-gm sc	1090	...	...	25¾	21½	24¼	− ⅝
89⅛	79	A-ek un							

Scores

In 1987, a steady progression of Prospectuses were issued creating a new type of "Warrant." The quotation marks denote that these Warrants had very special

August 24, 1987

52-Weeks High	Low	Name and Dividend	Sales 100s	Yield Pct.	P/E Ratio	Week's High	Low	Last	Net Chg.	
67	54½	A-ek pr	36	...	...	66½	64¾	66	− ¼	✚
38	18¼	A-ek sc	397	...	...	38	35¼	38	+ 1	
...	...	A-f un2.95	...	...	...	...	...	...	...	
69¾	61½	A-f pr 2.95	37	4.3	...	69½	67¾	68½	− 1	
43	27	A-f sc	690	...	...	u43	40⅜	41	− 1	
...	...	A-jnj un	...	...	...	...	...	...	...	
63¾	61¼	A-jnj pr	x85	...	...	u63¾	62⅜	63¾	+ 2	
41⅝	37	A-jnj sc	172	...	...	41¼	38½	40⅞	+ ⅞	
69	65½	A-hwp un.21	20	.3	...	65½	d65½	65½	− 3¼	
44¾	40⅜	A-hwp pr	186	...	...	42½	d40⅜	41¼	− 1¼	
27⅝	19⅞	A-hwp sc	711	...	...	u27⅝	23¾	27½	+ ½	
169½	159½	A-ibm un4.35	...	...	...	...	...	...	...	
132	121	A-ibm pr4.35	404	3.6	...	123¾	d121	121	− 1½	
56¼	36¼	A-ibm sc	1057	...	...	u56¼	49½	56	+ 4⅜	
188½	147¼	A-mrk un3.15	...	...	...	...	...	...	...	
137	105¾	A-mrk pr3.15	127	2.4	...	136½	132	132	− 4½	
75⅝	41⅜	A-mrk sc	878	...	...	u75⅝	69	72	+ 3¾	
...	...	A-3m un	...	...	...	...	...	...	...	
...	...	A-3m pr	...	...	...	...	...	...	...	
...	...	A-3m sc	...	...	...	...	...	...	...	
104⅛	104⅛	A-mo un	...	...	...	...	...	...	...	
71½	68	A-mo pr	60	...	...	u71½	69¼	71½	+ 1⅛	
42⅝	29½	A-mo sc	1013	...	...	u42⅝	35	42⅝	+ 7	
52¾	50¼	A-mob un2.15	8	4.3	...	50¾	d50¼	50¼	− 1½	✚
39¾	37	A-mob pr2.15	90	5.7	...	37¾	d37	37⅝	− ⅜	✚
15⅞	12⅜	A-mob sc	88	...	...	14¼	13½	14¼	+ ¼	
96⅛	64½	A-pg un2.65	...	...	...	...	...	...	...	
70¾	62½	A-pg pr 2.65	51	3.8	...	69¾	68½	69½	− ¼	
34¾	24½	A-pg sc	172	...	...	33¾	31¼	33⅜	+ 1	
52	51⅜	A-s un1.95	...	...	...	...	...	...	...	
42½	38⅜	A-s pr 1.95	228	4.9	...	40⅝	39½	40	− ¾	
19½	12¼	A-s sc	861	...	...	19⅛	17½	18¾	+ ⅜	
...	...	A-tx un	...	...	...	...	...	...	...	
...	...	A-tx pr	...	...	...	...	...	...	...	
...	...	A-tx sc	...	...	...	...	...	...	...	
75¼	74⅞	A-unp un1.95	...	...	...	...	...	...	...	
57	51½	A-unp pr1.95	71	3.5	...	56	54¾	55¼	− 1	
29¾	19¼	A-unp sc	117	...	...	27½	25½	26¾	− ½	
82	73½	A-xrx un	5	...	...	u82	82	82	+ 8½	
60	56½	A-xrx pr	50	...	...	58½	d56½	57	− 2⅝	
28¾	15	A-xrx sc	503	...	...	u28¾	24¼	28¾	+ 4¼	

characteristics, all of which we shall soon explain, but, to begin with, let us understand that, as with all Warrants, they were highly-*leveraged.* This factor was very important because these Warrants, called "Scores," represented the right to buy ***26 of the very top blue chips on the New York Stock Exchange.*** All Scores trade on the American Stock Exchange, and we shall begin by

BARRON'S January 4, 1988

American Stock Exchange

52-Weeks High	Low	Name and Dividend	Sales 100s	Yield Pct.	P/E Ratio	Week's High	Low	Last	Net Chg.
38⅞	21⅜	A-axp un .71	4	3.0	...	23½	22	23½	+ 2⅛
27¼	16½	A-axp pr .71	443	3.7	..	19⅜	18½	19¼	+ ⅜
14	3⅝	A-axp sc	421	.	...	4⅝	4⅛	4¼	− ½
92½	65¼	A-ahp un3.29	...	...	...	...	...	...	...
70	53	A-ahp pr3.29	10	5.3	...	62	60½	62	+ ½
26	8	A-ahp sc	335	...	...	10½	8⅞	10¼	+ ¼
35½	23¼	A-att2 un1.15	1	4.3	..	27	27	27	− 1⅜
23⅝	18⅛	A-att2 pr1.15	694	5.5	..	20¾	20⅜	20¾	....
14⅞	4	A-att2 sc	1219		...	7⅜	6¾	7	− ⅛
90	64⅝	A-an un3.25	...	...	...	...	...	...	...
68½	47	A-an pr 3.25	134	5.3	.	61	59	61	+ 2
30¼	5	A-an sc	108		...	9¼	7½	8¼	+ ⅛
98¼	88¾	A-arc un3.95	...	...	...	...	...	...	...
78⅛	56¾	A-arc pr3.95	9	6.5	..	62	61	61	+ 2
23¾	8¼	A-arc sc	33	.	...	10	9½	9½	− ⅝
110	75	A-bmy un2.75	4	3.2		86	84	86	− 2
75½	50	A-bmy pr2.75	51	3.9	...	71	68⅛	70½	− 1½
36¾	12½	A-bmy sc	265	..	.	16	13¾	13¾	− 2¾
61¾	38⅜	A-chv un2.35	...	...	...	...	...	...	...
52	24	A-chv pr2.35	127	6.7	..	36	34⅞	35	− ½
17½	3¼	A-chv sc	194		..	5¼	4½	4½	− ¾
56½	38½	A-ko un1.07	...	...	...	...	...	...	...
34	27¾	A-ko pr 1.07	295	3.3	.	33¼	32	32	− ½
26½	7½	A-ko sc	379	.	...	8¼	d 7½	7¾	− ⅝
86½	73⅛	A-dow un2.15	...	...	...	...	...	...	...
72	45	A-dow pr2.15	3	3.0	..	71½	69½	71½	+ 1⅜
44¼	14¾	A-dow sc	191		...	20	18¾	19¾	− ⅝

pointing out that each Score is found in the table as A-followed by the symbol of the blue chip, followed by "sc." Thus, the **IBM** Score is carried as A- ibm sc, the **General Electric** Score is carried as A-ge sc etc. We shall shortly list all the blue chips with their symbols, so that they may be easily found. We next point to the *date* of the first two pages of tables (all tables courtesy of **Barron's**), and, as can be expected, with late-August 1987 about the *top* of the pre-crash market, all the Scores were elevated in price. The next set of tables is dated *January 4, 1988,* and gives the close for *December 31, 1987*, which was near the low after the October 1987 market crash, and the Scores have been hit *very* hard. The High-Low tables tell the story, and we will name

January 4, 1988

52-Weeks High	52-Weeks Low	Name and Dividend	Sales 100s	Yield Pct.	P/E Ratio	Week's High	Week's Low	Week's Last	Net Chg.
128⅝	77	A-dd un 3.35	2	3.9	...	86½	86½	86½	+ 1½
80½	60	A-dd pr 3.35	13	4.7	...	72	71½	72	− ½
49¾	13¼	A-dd sc	165	...	...	16	14¾	15⅛	− ¾
99½	73⅜	A-xon un3.95							
60½	56	A-xon pr3.95	854	6.7	...	59	58½	59	......
40⅝	14¾	A-xon sc	948	...	...	20½	18	18⅛	− 3⅜
45⅜	32	A-gte un2.47	35	7.1	...	35	35	35	− 1⅞
34	27	A-gte pr2.47	496	8.0	...	31½	30½	31	......
13	3⅜	A-gte sc	1426	...	...	5⅜	4¾	5⅜	+ ⅛
131½	81	A-ge un2.75							
89	64	A-ge pr 2.75	28	3.7	...	75½	74	75	− 1
49	12¾	A-ge sc	178	...	...	16¼	14⅝	14⅞	− 1⅝
92	56¼	A-gm un4.95	3	8.1	...	61¼	61¼	61¼	− ¾
71¾	45½	A-gm pr4.95	47	8.9	...	55¾	54⅝	55⅜	+ ⅛
26	5⅝	A-gm sc	426	...	...	7⅜	6½	6½	− 1⅜
104½	71¼	A-ek un2.65							
67	50½	A-ek pr 2.65	19	4.6	...	57½	56¼	57½	− ⅛
46⅜	14½	A-ek sc	137	...	...	17¼	16	16⅝	− 1⅜
110	75⅝	A-f un3.95							
69¾	50	A-f pr 3.95	67	6.5	...	61½	60	61	− ⅞
43	12½	A-f sc	305	...	...	16¾	14½	14¾	− 2¾
101	69½	A-jnj un1.63							
66⅛	52	A-jnj pr 1.63	18	2.6	...	63	62½	62⅝	− ⅞
42¼	11⅝	A-jnj sc	69	...	...	15½	13¼	13½	− 2⅜
69	50⅜	A-hwp un.21							
44¾	29½	A-hwp pr.21	10	.5	...	42	40	42	......
30¾	10⅝	A-hwp sc	63	...	...	16⅝	15⅜	15⅜	− 1⅜
169½	113½	A-ibm un4.35							
132	88½	A-ibm pr4.35	183	4.5	...	96¾	95½	96¾	− 1½
58	14⅛	A-ibm sc	567	..	...	21½	19½	19½	− 2½
217	147¼	A-mrk un3.15							
138	96½	A-mrk pr3.15	122	2.9	...	108	103	108	+ 1½
87½	41⅜	A-mrk sc	142	...	...	55⅞	54	54	− 2
116	84	A-mo un3.55	4	4.1	..	87	86	86	− 2
77	57	A-mo pr3.55	33	5.4	...	67	65⅞	65⅞	− 1¾
51¾	20	A-mo sc	73	...	...	22	20½	20½	− 2½
52¾	34½	A-mob un2.15							
39¾	27½	A-mob pr2.15	113	6.5	...	33⅝	33	33¼	− ⅜
19	4¾	A-mob sc	150	...	...	6	5⅜	5⅝	− ⅜
98	64½	A-pg un2.65							
70¾	56½	A-pg pr 2.65	5	3.9	...	68	66½	67½	......
37½	13¾	A-pg sc	26	...	...	18⅜	16¾	16¾	− 2
53⅜	30⅝	A-s un 1.95	6	5.6	...	34¾	33½	34¾	+ 4⅛
42½	26	A-s pr 1.95	319	6.7	...	30¼	28¾	29¼	− ⅝
20	4¼	A-s sc	627	...	...	5⅜	4⅞	5	− ¼
78¾	49½	A-unp un1.95							
57	37½	A-unp pr1.95	22	4.4	...	45¼	44	44	− 3
29¾	7¼	A-unp sc	75	...	...	10¾	9⅝	9⅝	− 1⅝
82	50¾	A-xrx un2.95							
60	42	A-xrx pr2.95	31	6.3	...	47½	47	47	− ¼
30	7	A-xrx sc	68	...	...	10	9¼	9¼	− ⅞

BARRON'S July 17, 1989

American Stock Exchange

52-Weeks High	52-Weeks Low	Name and Dividend	Sales 100s	Yield Pct.	P/E Ratio	Week's High	Week's Low	Last	Net Chg.
35¾	26	A-axp un .79	1	2.2	..	u35¾	35¾	35¾	+ 2½
30¼	22¾	A-axp .79	162	2.7	...	u30¼	29	29¾	+ 1
7½	2¾	A-axp sc	1408	.	..	6⅝	6	6¼	+ ⅛
96½	73	A-ahp un3.85	7	4.0	...	u96½	96	96½	+ 1⅞
75½	65¼	A-ahp 3.85	37	5.1	..	u75½	74½	75⅛	+ ⅞
24⅜	8¾	A-ahp sc	389	...	..	23	21½	22¼	+ ¼
37¾	25	A-att2 un1.15	655	3.0	...	u37¾	36¼	37¾	+ ⅞
25⅞	20¾	A-att2 1.15	895	4.5	. .	u25⅞	25	25¾	+ ⅝
12⅞	4⅛	A-att2 sc	2005	..	..	12⅜	11⅜	12	+ ⅛
88	73	A-an un3.75	...	...	...	...	...	...	...
82	64¼	A-an 3.75	4	4.6	..	u82	82	82	+ 1
12⅝	4½	A-an sc	372	...	...	u12⅝	11¼	11⅝	+ ½
92½	76¾	A-arc un4.45	...	...	...	...	...	...	...
84	70⅝	A-arc 4.45	86	5.3	.	u84	82¼	83¾	+ 2¼
14½	5½	A-arc sc	371	...	.	u14½	12¾	13¼	+ ⅞
103	79	A-bmy un3.95	...	...	...	...	...	...	...
84½	70	A-bmy 3.95	64	4.8	...	83¾	82¾	83	+ ½
20⅛	8½	A-bmy sc	296	..	..	18¼	17	17⅞	+ 1⅛
54½	43⅜	A-chv un2.75	...	...	...	...	...	...	...
49¾	40⅛	A-chv 2.75	55	5.6	..	49¾	48½	49⅛	+ ⅝
7⅜	2¾	A-chv sc	572	..	.	u 7⅜	6¾	7	.. ..
60	36	A-ko un 1.31	1	2.2	.	59¼	59¼	59¼	+ 2⅜
43⅛	32	A-ko 1.31	89	3.0	.	u43⅛	42⅛	43	+ 1
18½	4⅜	A-ko sc	394	..	...	17⅛	15⅞	16¼	− ½
99½	82¾	A-dow un3.15	...	...	...	...	...	...	...
83	68	A-dow 3.15	129	4.3		75	73¼	73⅞	+ ⅝
22⅜	11⅞	A-dow sc	617	..	.	17½	15¼	16⅞	+ 1⅞
112¾	79¾	A-dd un 4.15	4	3.7	..	111¼	110¾	111¼	+ 2
88¾	69¼	A-dd 4.15	50	4.7	..	u88¾	87⅜	87⅞	+ ⅜
28	7⅛	A-dd sc	813	.	.	25⅞	23⅝	25½	+ 1⅝
93¾	84	A-xon un4.35	...	...	...	...	...	...	...
60½	56½	A-xon 4.35	62	7.3	...	60	59⅞	60	.....
34½	24	A-xon sc	420	...	..	30½	28½	30½	+ 2
58	39	A-gte un2.63	4	4.5	.	u58	56¼	58	+ 2⅜
40¼	33	A-gte 2.63	173	6.6	..	u40¼	39	40	+ 1⅜
18¼	5	A-gte sc	1883		.	18	16½	17¾	+ 1⅜
109½	78	A-ge un3.23	...	...	...	...	...	...	...
95¾	72	A-ge 3.23	55	3.4	.	u95¾	93⅛	95	+ 1¾
20½	6¾	A-ge sc	388			17¼	16	17	+ ⅝
91¼	72⅛	A-gm un5.95	...	...	...	...	...	...	...
79⅞	64¾	A-gm 5.95	186	7.8		76	72½	76	+ 3½
15¼	6	A-gm sc	696			11	9⅜	11	+ 1½

just a few. The **Amoco** Score (an) has dropped from 30.25 to 5.00, the **Coca-Cola** Score (ko) has dropped from 26.50 to 7.50, the **Du Pont** Score (dd) has dropped from 49.75 to 13.25, the **General Electric** Score (ge) has dropped from 49.00 to 12.75, the **IBM** Score (ibm) has dropped from 58 to 14.12, and so it goes throughout the

July 17, 1989

52-Weeks High	52-Weeks Low	Name and Dividend	Sales 100s	Yield Pct.	P/E Ratio	Week's High	Week's Low	Last	Net Chg.	
79	62½	A-ek un 2.95	8	3.8	.	78½	76¼	78½	+ 2¼	
64⅞	55¾	A-ek 2.95	565	4.8	..	61½	59¾	61⅛	+ ¾	
19⅝	5½	A-ek sc	1970	.	.	17⅜	14⅝	16⅞	+ 1¼	
104⅛	93¾	A-f un5.95	...	...	...	...	...	...	...	
87¼	76	A-f 5.95	158	7.2	..	83	80½	83	+ 2½	
26⅛	15¼	A-f sc	400	.	...	17½	16½	17¼	+ ½	
103	77	A-jnj un 1.95	6	2.0	..	103	99½	99½	− 3½	
82	67	A-jnj 1.95	139	2.5	..	80½	77½	78		
29½	7½	A-jnj sc	208	..	.	23⅜	22½	22¾	− ¼	
56¼	46½	A-hwp un.29	...	...	...	...	...	...	...	
51¼	38½	A-hwp .29	267	.6	..	45	44	44¾	+ ½	
10¾	5½	A-hwp sc	203	. .	...	9⅛	8½	8⅝	− ½	
129½	108	A-ibm un4.79	...	...	...	...	...	...	...	
117½	99¼	A-ibm 4.79	373	4.6	..	104¾	102½	104½	+ 1⅞	
13⅞	9⅛	A-ibm sc	5294	. .	. .	12	11⅛	11½	+ ⅜	
214½	162	A-mrk un4.87	...	...	...	...	...	...	...	
158½	131½	A-mrk 4.87	102	3.1	..	u158½	155½	158	+ 4½	
64½	27	A-mrk sc	470	.	..	57¾	55⅝	57	+ 1⅜	
153	89	A-mo un4.45	4	2.9	..	u153	151	151	+ 3	
91½	71½	A-mo 4.45	46	4.9	.	u91½	90	91	+ ⅞	
64¼	14½	A-mo sc	2278	.	.	u64¼	59¾	61⅝	+ ⅞	
51	40⅞	A-mob un2.55	...	...	...	...	...	...	...	
45	38⅛	A-mob 2.55	121	5.8	..	44⅞	43¾	44	+ ¼	
8¾	3⅝	A-mob sc	488	.	...	8½	7⅝	8⅛	...	
113	71½	A-pg un3.15	...	...	...	...	...	...	...	✚
85¼	65	A-pg 3.15	72	3.7	.	u85¼	82¾	85⅛	+ 2⅜	✚
33½	7¼	A-pg sc	451	.	.	32	29¼	32	+ 2¼	
47⅛	35	A-s un1.95	...	...	...	...	...	...	...	
41½	32	A-s 1.95	56	5.1	.	39¼	38¼	38¼	− ⅝	
7½	3	A-s sc	1257		..	6⅞	6	6⅛	− ⅝	
72¾	57	A-unp un2.15	10	3.0	..	72	72	72	− ¼	
60¾	49¾	A-unp 2.15	68	3.6	...	60	59½	59½	+ ½	
15	5¾	A-unp sc	54	.	.	13½	13	13½	+ ½	
68	52½	A-xrx un2.95	1	4.5	.	66¼	66¼	66¼	+ 2¼	✚
61	48½	A-xrx 2.95	146	5.1	..	58¼	55¾	58	+ 2	✚
9⅜	3⅝	A-xrx sc	890			9⅜	8¾	8⅞	+ ⅛	

list. *Now*, to observe *up*side leverage thus far, look at the tables dated *July 17, 1989*, which gives the close for *July 14, 1989*, a recovery high. The **American Home Products** Score (ahp) has advanced from 8.75 to 24.37, the **Atlantic Richfield** Score (arc) has advanced from 5.50 to 14.50, the **Du Pont** Score (dd) has advanced from 7.12 to 28.00, the **Eastman Kodak** Score (ek) has advanced from 5.50 to 19.62, the **Philip Morris** Score (mo) has advanced from 14.50 to 64.25 and the **Procter & Gamble** Score (pg) has advanced from 7.25 to 33.50.

Since we expect *large* market swings to come in subsequent markets, including a *deep* market decline, to be followed by a new bull market, it is obvious that the reader will want to know *all about* Scores, and how they provide such a leveraged response to movement of their blue chip common stocks. What follows aims at supplying that knowledge.

Scores (Warrants) On 26 Top Blue Chips

In exactly the same time period:

Du Pont common moved from
79 to 105 . . . . .up *33 %*

while the **Du Pont Score**
moved from 7-1/8 to 23-7/8 . . . . .up *235 %*

Why did the Du Pont Score *advance 7 times faster* than Du Pont common?

This, of course, is nothing unusual for a *Warrant*, as we have certainly demonstrated in our discussion of Eli Lilly Warrants, General Tire & Rubber Warrants, Capital Cities/ABC Warrants, and other Warrants. But they were all "American-style" Warrants, which could be exchanged for common stock at any time up to expiration date, whereas the Du Pont "Score" was a "European-style" Warrant, where the Warrant could be exchanged for common stock *only on the last day of its life,* which was years hence.

The Du Pont Score was nevertheless able to advance sharply, because of the way it was created — and that creation included something called an "Americus Trust" and a "Prime" *along with* the Score. A remarkable speculative medium, with high promise of capital appreciation was created when "Americus Trust," "Prime" and "Score" came into being, so let us explain the whole process from the beginning, before we get into what we deem to be the high profit potential for investors who understand how to use these new market instruments.

The creation of a new investment entity is never initiated from an altruistic viewpoint — it comes about because *there is profit in it*. And, first and foremost, the Americus Trust concept came into being because the institutional investors and funds that held the blue chip stocks, the individuals who conceived the approach, and the investment banking houses that brought the concept to life, all expected to make money, each in their own way.

A. Joseph Debe and his company were among the prime movers of the concept, and Alex Brown & Sons was the investment banker for almost all of the Trusts, and the back cover of each Prospectus set forth what had been created, in condensed form, the example shown being for the Du Pont Americus Trust. (See next page.)

As each Prospectus spelled out, the intent was to take a blue chip share of stock and break it down into two components, one component representing the right to receive dividends, and the other component representing

**Americus Trust
for Du Pont
Shares**

SPONSOR:

**Americus Shareowner
Service Corp.**

DEALER MANAGER

Alex. Brown & Sons
Incorporated

the right to the capital appreciation that might be expected to flow from the investment.

Towards this end, large holders of blue chips — basically institutional holders — were approached to exchange shares of blue chip common stocks for Units in an Americus Trust.

A separate Americus Trust was set up for each successful offer, which would hold the blue chip shares tendered and exchange each share for one Americus Trust Unit which consisted of one Prime and one Score. The Unit certificates could be immediately separated, the holder able to sell off either the Prime or the Score, and retain the part that was desired.

And all three parts, the Unit itself, the Prime and the Score would trade separately on the American Stock Exchange, providing a market for any later approach desired.

The *Prime* was the income component of the Unit, entitled to receive all dividends paid. Such dividend payments were made by the blue chip company to the Americus Trust for that stock, since the original shares tendered were now owned by the Trust, and when the Trust received the dividends, they would pay them out to the holders of the Primes, retaining only 5 cents per share per annum, to meet the modest expenses of the Trust.

The Score was not entitled to receive any dividends, but would receive all appreciation in the common stock beyond a stated price, in a manner we shall now describe.

Each Americus Trust had a stated life of five years,

which the Prospectus calls the "Termination Date." We happen to be looking at the Prospectus for the "Americus Trust for IBM Shares," and on the third page of the Prospectus, the "Termination Date Of The Trust" is given as June 30, 1992.

There is also something called the *"Termination Claim,"* and it is the price therein stated which gives meaning to Prime and Score as the underlying common stock fluctuates in the marketplace.

Thus, the Termination Claim for the IBM Americus Trust is *$210*, which has relevance as follows: On June 30, 1992, the Americus Trust for IBM shares will go out of business, and its assets (almost all assets consisting of the original shares of IBM that had been tendered) would be distributed to the holders of Primes and Scores.

Each Prime would be entitled to receive assets up to the Termination Claim which, remember, was $210. Thus, if IBM common was selling *at* 210 on the Termination Date (June 30, 1992), each Prime would get value in IBM stock of $210, which would account for all the shares available for distribution, while the Score would receive nothing.

If IBM common was selling *below* 210 on the Termination Date, the Primes would still be getting all the shares, but they would be worth whatever the market price of IBM happened to be on that Termination Date, while the Scores would still get nothing.

If, however, IBM common was selling *above* 210 on the Termination Date, the Prime would get its *maximum* value in IBM shares of 210 — and *the Score would get all the rest.*

Thus, if IBM common would be selling at *300* on the Termination Date, the Prime would get only its maximum of 210 in value, while the Score would get the difference, or $90 in value.

This, of course, is what makes the Score a *Warrant,* since it has a specific life (to the Termination Date), and a specific exercise price (the Termination Claim). Where the Score differs from an American Warrant is that the American Warrant, in almost all instances, can be exchanged for common stock (exercised) at *any* time, while the Score can be exercised only on the Termination Date of the applicable Americus Trust.

At this point, we go back to the beginning and consider the question as to *why* an institutional holder would be willing to exchange blue chip shares for Prime/Score Units in the first place.

Take such an institutional holder that was primarily interested in the dividend yield, and only secondarily in the possible appreciation of the stock, and consider that they could tender the shares, sell off the Scores, retain the Primes, and thereby put themselves in an excellent position, as follows:

The Prime was entitled to the same dividend as the common stock, less the miniscule five cents per share per annum, but in selling off the Score, the *cost* of the Prime was now less than the common stock.

We can see what this means by looking at the price of IBM common stock, as we are writing, and the price of the IBM Prime, on the American Stock Exchange. IBM common closed at 120-7/8, and pays dividends of $4.40 for the year, while the IBM Prime closed at 110-1/4 and pays $4.35 for the year.

The yield on the common stock is 3.64%, while the yield on the Prime is 3.95%. This might not seem like much incentive for a speculatively minded investor interested in building capital, but to an institutional investor to whom return on invested capital is supremely important, that difference in yield is quite significant. Further, the funds received upon originally selling the Score could be invested in additional Primes, which would increase the return still further.

And would giving up appreciation potential beyond the $210 Termination Claim dissuade the institutional investor? Not in most cases, since IBM moving from 120-7/8 to 210 would be *quite* satisfactory from a conservatively approached investment standpoint.

So the institutional investor who originally tendered shares was, from that point of view, very comfortably situated with the remaining Primes, receiving the considerably higher yield for the 5-year life of the Americus Trust, and still guaranteed the substantial capital gain, if the stock went up from the price where the shares were tendered to the Termination Claim five years hence.

And the exchange of blue chip stock for the Americus Trust Unit was ruled by the Internal Revenue Service to be a tax-free exchange. Responding to all of the above logic, Americus Trusts for *26* blue chip stocks were successfully launched, and below we give the salient information on those 26 Americus Trusts.

Name	Term Date	Term Price
American Express (axp)	8-92	50.00
Amer Home Prod (ahp)	12-91	90.00
A T & T (att)	2-92	30.00
Amoco (an)	3-92	105.00
Atl Richfield (arc)	7-92	116.00
Bristol-Myers (bmy)	2-92	110.00
Chevron (chv)	7-92	75.00
Coca-Cola (ko)	7-92	56.00
Dow Chemical (dow)	5-92	110.00
Du Pont (dd)	3-92	110.00
Eastman Kodak (ek)	3-92	92.00

WARRANTS, OPTIONS and CONVERTIBLES

Name	Term Date	Term Price
Exxon (xon)	9.90	60.00
Ford (f)	6-92	104.00
GTE (gte)	7-92	44.00
General Electric (ge)	5-92	140.00
General Motors (gm)	6-92	107.00
Hewlett-Packard (hwp)	7-92	90.00
IBM (ibm)	6-92	210.00
John & John (jnj)	6-92	118.00
Merck (mrk)	4-92	200.00
Mobil (mob)	6-92	60.00
Philip Morris (mo)	7-92	110.00
Procter & Gamble (pg)	6-92	105.00
Sears (s)	7-92	64.00

Name	Term Date	Term Price
Union Pacific (unp)	4-92	87.00
Xerox (xrx)	7-92	97.00

The Profit Potential Of The Americus Trust Scores

If the Score was not exerciseable for the underlying common stock until the Termination Date, it would not be such a remarkable investment instrument. But, in what we consider to be a stroke of genius, the originators of the whole concept, with Mr. Debe in the forefront, instituted a provision which applies to each and every Americus Trust, the provision stating that *at any time*, one Prime plus one Score could be turned in to the appropriate Americus Trust, and *be exchanged for one share of common stock*.

This made each Score a truly exciting vehicle for capital appreciation, on a par with any American-style Warrant, and, indeed, even more so, because the Scores represented Warrants on 26 top blue chips, which we enumerated in the table previously presented.

It is important that the reader follow the reasoning carefully, as to *why* the Scores have become so promising, because of this provision. We will use the example of the **Du Pont Score** for our explanation.

To begin with, for at least the time period since the October 1987 crash, when Scores were driven down to quite low price levels, the equation has persisted in unanimous fashion for *all* the Prime/Score situations, that one Prime plus one Score just about equals the current price of the underlying common stock.

To demonstrate this, we look at closing prices for a representative selection of Common/Prime/Score for July 26, 1989, do the necessary arithmetic, and once again make the findings (we have checked this many times on previous occasions) that the current prices of one Prime plus one Score does indeed approximately equal the common stock price.

Name	Prime	Score	Prime plus Score	Common
Amer Exp	29.87	6.37	36.25	35.50
A T & T	25.87	14.37	40.28	39.37
Coca-Cola	45.00	18.87	63.87	63.62
Dow Chem	75.12	18.25	93.37	90.75
Du Pont	88.75	26.62	115.37	115.00
GTE	39.87	17.87	57.75	57.87
Hlt Pack	44.75	8.12	52.87	52.12

If we go back to the November 1988 prices for Du Pont common, Prime and Score, we can see this "equation" in operation.

Du Pont *common* was then selling at 79, the Du Pont *Prime* was selling at 72-1/8 and the Du Pont *Score* was selling at 7-1/8.

Add 72-1/8 and 7-1/8 and you get 79-1/4, only 1/4 point more than Du Pont common.

And in our observation throughout, for all the 26 blue chips with Primes/Scores trading, the combination of Prime plus Score prices has always just about equaled the common stock price.

Now it is necessary to understand *why* the Du Pont Score went from 7-1/8 to 23-7/8, up 235%, when Du Pont common went from 79 to 105, up 33%, the Score advancing 7 times faster than Du Pont common, and to do that we must understand what makes a *Prime* attractive, or less attractive, for purchase.

To begin with, as we have noted in previous paragraphs, the Prime gets the same dividend as the common stock (less that 5 cents fee), but *sells at a lower price* than the common stock; hence the yield is larger. The advantage may be only 1% or so, but to those who invest for yield — particularly institutional investors — that 1% can be quite important.

At this point, it will be useful for the reader to look at the next two pages which show Du Pont common and the Du Pont Score facing one another. Both charts are courtesy of **Daily Graphs.**

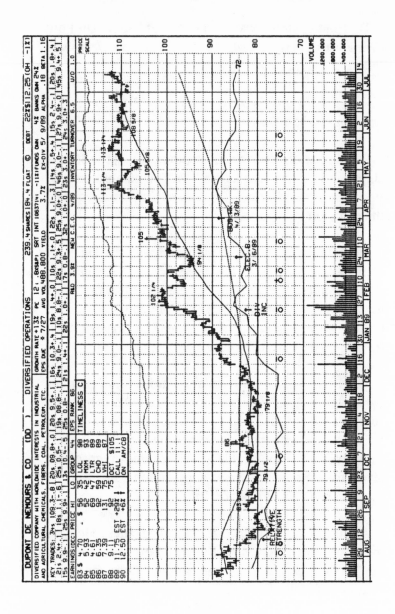

230

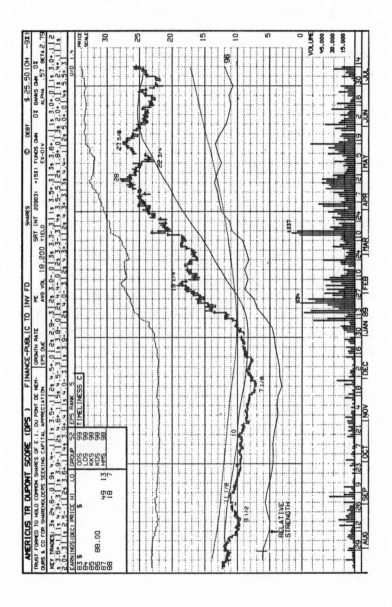

231

The reader should take note of the fact that although Du Pont common and the Du Pont Score *seemed* to parallel one another in moving to the upside, we are talking of a common stock which reached the *110* area, and a Score which reached the *25* area. The *leverage* of the well-selected Score is very clear.

Continuing now with our discussion of the Du Pont Prime and Score, we look at the most important factor: the hoped-for capital gain when Termination Date arrives and the assets of the Americus Trust are distributed among Prime and Score.

Recall that the Prime is entitled to receive *up to* the Termination Claim price. If, then, the common stock and, therefore, the Prime, are selling considerably *below* the Termination Claim price, the potential for capital gain is *large*, making it attractive for purchase, while if the Prime is selling *much closer* to the Termination Claim price, the capital gain potential is *smaller*, making the Prime that much *less* attractive for purchase.

In the case of Du Pont in November 1988, the Prime was selling at 72-1/8 while the Termination Claim price was $110. As Du Pont common rose in December 1988 and January 1989, and in the months following, the Prime rose as well, but as Du Pont came closer and closer to the $110 Termination Claim price, the capital gain potential of the Prime (the difference between the Termination Claim price and the Prime price), became *less and less*, so the Prime rose less and less rapidly in relation to the common.

Since the "equation" reads: one Prime plus one Score just about equals one share of common stock, if the Prime *lagged* the common stock in its advance, the *Score* must make up the difference, which means *advancing more rapidly.*

That is why, between November 1988 - March 1989:

Du Pont common rose from 79 to 105   . . . up   33 %

Du Pont *Prime* rose
from 72-1/8 to 82-1/4   . . . up   14 %

while the Du Pont *Score*
rose from 7-1/8 to 23-7/8   . . . up 235 %

A Valuable Measuring Tool For Scores

What we have just described for Du Pont common, Prime and Score is one of the most important factors affecting this relatively new market instrument.

If the common stock is a considerable distance from the Termination Price, we would expect the Prime to keep pace with the common stock on any upside move, thereby giving the *Score* only limited scope for an appreciable advance.

If, on the other hand, as we saw in the late-1988 -early-1989 months with Du Pont, the common stock *approaches* the Termination Price by dint of a substantial rise, then we should become very interested in the Score, because any *further* rise in the common stock would find the Prime lagging in *its* advance, while the Score *must* advance, close to point-for-point with the common stock, giving it the kind of excellent leverage that we saw demonstrated with the Du Pont Score.

Because this factor is so important, from time to time, we present the table shown on the opposite page, in the pages of the **R.H.M. Survey,** in which we calculate the common stock price *as a percentage of the Termination Price.*

The closer the individual Americus Trust is to the top of the table, the more likely it is that *the Prime will lag,* and the *Score* will begin to move rapidly to the upside on a percentage basis, if the common stock continues to move higher.

This does not mean that the Americus Trust Scores near the middle or the bottom of the list are to be ig-

SCORES

Name	Common Price	Termination Price	Com Price As % Of Termin. Pr.
Exxon	89.50*	60.00	149.16%
Ford	105.25*	104.00	101.20%
GTE	44.37	44.00	100.85%
A T & T	29.00	30.00	96.67%
Philip Morris	102.75	110.00	93.41%
American Home Products	81.87	90.00	91.00%
Merck	181.87*	200.00	90.94%
Proctor & Gamble	87.37	105.00	83.21%
Du Pont	91.50	110.00	83.18%
General Motors	87.87	107.00	82.13%
Dow Chemical	89.62	110.00	81.48%
Bristol-Myers	88.50*	110.00	80.45%
Coca-Cola	44.50	56.00	79.46%
Mobil	47.62	60.00	79.38%
Union Pacific	67.12	87.00	77.16%
Amoco	78.12	105.00	74.40%
Eastman Kodak	67.31*	92.00	73.16%
Atlantic Richfield	84.50	116.00	72.84%
Johnson & Johnson	85.37	118.00	72.35%
Sears	41.75	64.00	65.23%
Chevron	48.50	75.00	64.67%
General Electric	89.75*	140.00	64.11%
Xerox	59.12	97.00	60.95%
IBM	124.25	210.00	59.17%
Hewlett-Packard	52.50	90.00	58.33%
American Express	27.87	50.00	55.75%

nored. The kind of moderate, even *gentle*, fluctuation they will provide, with the similar fluctuation of the common stock, could be quite valuable in *profitable trading techniques.* We will discuss that further in a later page, when we will have something to say about a *very* "gentle" mover — the *IBM Score.*

Lessons Of The American Tel & Tel Score

Every one of the 26 blue chip stocks for which Scores are trading is important for analysis, either because of current opportunities, or opportunities that could develop in the near future.

What follows now on the *American Tel & Tel Score* is meant to give the reader some idea of how such a situation is analyzed, in much the same manner that we analyzed *Equitable Resources* in the Warrant segment of this book.

In the Survey issue of May 27, 1988, we headed our comments with "A T & T — A Score BUY Recommendation," and stated that " . . . purchases should start now, at current levels of 5.50."

In doing so, we gave our estimate that " . . . we see A T & T common reaching about the *$70 per share level* over those coming few years," the last part referring to the fact we had noted that the Americus Trust for A T & T has a Termination Date of February 1992. (Original emphasis).

With a Termination Price of *30*, that would make the

Score worth *40*, if the common would sell at 70, and in a full write-up dated June 3, 1988 (one week after the initial recommendation) we gave the background for the Buy rating, under the heading: "Why the A T & T Score Is A Superlative 'Buy.' "

We described how, on January 1, 1984, American Tel & Tel had spun off 22 Bell operating companies, leaving A T & T with about 23% of the assets of the old company, which included the long distance communications business, the manufacture of telecommunications equipment, and the selling and servicing of that equipment.

The *positive factors* that we saw included the fact that the telecommunications business was "about a $500 billion market worldwide, and is estimated to be growing at about 8% a year for equipment and services."

With A T & T the world leader in that field, by a wide margin, and with an annual cash flow of about $5 billion each year, constituting a "war chest" with which to pursue a *dominant* role in that business, we stated our strong belief that revenues and earnings would be moving much higher, year-by-year.

As the months went by, following that recommendation, more and more favorable news kept coming out about A T & T. 1988 saw $1.8 billion earned on its long distance business, which worked out to about a 20% return on equity. With the company introducing efficiencies that were expected to pull that return up to the 30% mark, the outlook for earnings growth was looking even better. A Fiber-Optic Trans-Atlantic Service went

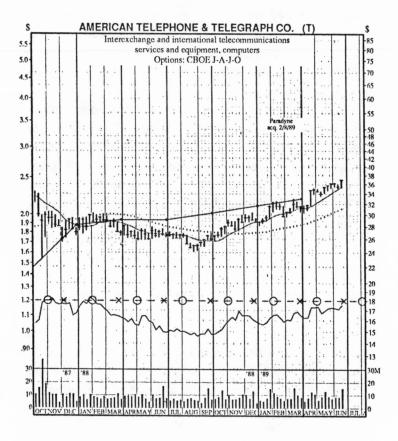

AMERICAN TELEPHONE & TELEGRAPH CO. (T)
Interexchange and international telecommunications
services and equipment, computers
Options: CBOE J-A-J-O

Paradyne
acq. 2/8/89

into operation that the company stated would eventually bring advanced telephone services to most of Europe, North America and East Asia, and this would allow multinational businesses to move computer data at high speeds between their offices in Europe and the United States.

In September 1988, A T & T common started moving

238

steadily higher, and has continued this progress to this writing. The chart shown (courtesy of **Securities Research**) shows the virtually uninterrupted climb of the common stock since August of 1988, and as we are writing, on July 27, 1989, A T & T common stock has made a new high at 40-5/8, up 1-1/4 points, and this follows the price action of the *previous* day, when it rose 1 point.

Emphasizing what we previously discussed about a *lag* in the Prime once the common stock was close to the Termination Price, on *both* days, the Prime did very little. Indeed, on the day that A T & T rose a full point, the Prime *slipped* by 1/8 point, and when A T & T common advanced another 1-1/4 point, the Prime got that 1/8 point back by advancing to that extent. So the upshot was that in a two-day 2-1/4 point gain by A T & T common stock, the Prime moved not at all!

In complete contrast, for those two days, the A T & T *Score* rose 1 point and 3/4 point respectively, or 1-3/4 point total, to a new high of 15-1/8. A gain of 2-1/4 points for the common, and 1-3/4 points for the Score, and it becomes quite clear that the Score is gaining not much less than point-for-point with the common stock. And this is exactly what logic tells us it *should* be doing, when the common advances and the Prime lags.

Since we are dealing here with a common now at 40-5/8, and a Score at 15-1/8, the fact that the Score is almost keeping pace with the common, point-for-point, translates into *high leverage.* This means that *whenever* the reader is planning to buy one of the 26 blue chips which have Americus Trusts in place, the relative prices of common, Prime and Score must be checked against the Termination Price.

In the case of A T & T, of course, the common stock has galloped far beyond the Termination Price, the latter being *30* whle the common is already at *40-5/8.* Anyone buying the Prime is getting a *higher dividend yield* than is true for the holder of the common stock, but is stuck at the 30 level where any hope of capital appreciation is considered. The *Score*, on the other hand, can look forward to getting *all* the appreciation beyond the Termination Price of *30*, and remember that we are looking for A T & T common to hit the *70* mark before Termination Date of February 1992 arrives!

With *any* of these blue chip Scores, then, if the common stock is selling close to the Termination Price, there is a *lot* of leverage in buying the Score rather than the common. Of course, the Score will also *decline* at a faster rate than the common stock, if that is where the common decides to go, but if one has very positive feelings about the company, the Score is where one should put one's investment. And after common and Score have retreated a bit, the Score will begin to show *less* percentage decline than the common, which will quickly become *much* less percentage decline. In such instances, the Score is *much* the better investment.

The IBM Score

Where the **A T & T Score** has turned in a magnificent performance because the common moved up sharply and was considerably above the Termination Price, the **IBM Score** has had only a mild trading range for the past year, because the common stock has traded in a narrow sideways Trend Channel and is *far below* the Termination Price.

Nevertheless, Scores that are in the position we have just outlined for the IBM Score *do* have profit potential, in different ways that we will be discussing below.

We will get to that shortly, but to begin with, let us take a look at IBM common stock itself, and first marvel at the fact that we are having a *large* stock market recovery *without* IBM, which must be rated as one ultimately negative feature for that market rise.

International Business Machines (IBM), of course, ranks number one in the world for the manufacture of data processing equipment and computer systems. In 1988, computer "hardware" sales contributed 67% of revenues, while "software" and the servicing of equipment was responsible for 29% of revenues. Foreign sales are vastly important for IBM, having contributed a whopping 71% of profits in 1988 on 58% of revenues.

The company leads its competitors in mainframe computers, but has much more competition in minicomputers, personal computers, and all the peripheral equipment which goes with the latter. Earnings have moved at a snail's pace in recent years, showing earnings of $10.67 per share in 1985, earnings below that level for

241

1986 through 1988, and is expected to finally get back to the 1985 level in 1989. While doing somewhat better on a cash flow basis, the results are still nothing to cheer about.

But the ponderous giant is getting its act together, and the early years of the new decade just ahead should see earnings move higher at a faster rate, but we must add that not all analysts feel that optimistic.

Having said that, we look at the long-term price chart for the common stock (courtesy of **Securities Research** — see next page) and note that there is no net price progress for the common stock since *1983*. The "Relative Strength" of the common stock (the line at the bottom of the chart) has been abysmal, IBM common lagging the rest of the market quite badly.

In light of all that, we now consider the fact that the IBM Americus Trust has a Termination Date of June 1992, and a Termination *Price* of *210*. With IBM common stock selling at 113 as we write (the high-low for the past 52 weeks being 130-7/8 - 106-1/4), this will cause the Prime to move up with the common stock, somewhat limiting the advance of the Score, unless there is a *pronounced* IBM common stock rise, which does not appear likely.

Having absorbed all of that, the reader should now take a careful look at the last 12 months of trading for the IBM Score (chart courtesy of **Daily Graphs** — see page 244), and note that each time the Score drops below the 10 level, it holds well, and then is able to make its way up to the 12 or 13 level on a minor rally in IBM common. 9-1/2 to 13 is not a bad trading profit, and

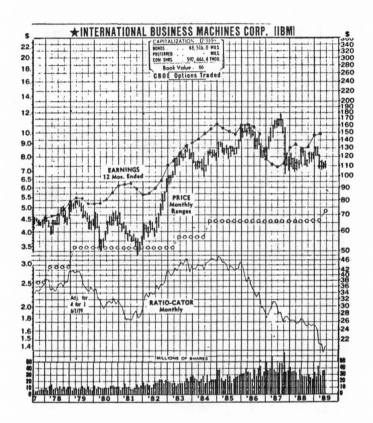

★INTERNATIONAL BUSINESS MACHINES CORP. (IBM)

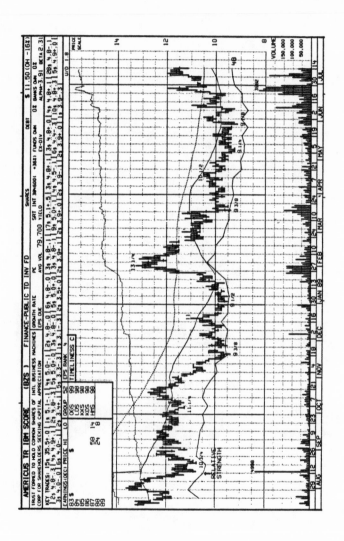

particularly when the downside loss potential is quite small, as we see it.

What we have just described is also true of *other* Scores, whose common/Prime/Score conditions parallel those of IBM, and such Scores are also candidates for small-risk trading profits.

One other potential for profit enters the picture, *which deserves the reader's attention.* The IBM *Score* is a *long-term* Call on the common stock. *Options on IBM common stock*, trading on the Chicago Board Options Exchange, have a life measured in *months*.

In such instances, there is always the possibility of a "Hedge" position, where you buy the long-lived Call (the Score) and sell short the Call Option that expires in some months.

The immediate rationale for that is the potential for the common stock not doing much of anything in the intervening period, causing the Option price to go to 0 while nothing much happens to the Score. Result? A very rewarding net profit!

Thus, **Barron's** for 7-24-89, covering market results for the week ending 7-21-89, tells us that IBM *common* traded at 116-3/4 high, 112-1/2 low, 114-1/8 close, while the *Score* had a high of 12-1/2, a low of 11-7/8 and a close at 12-1/2.

When we now look at the record of the week's trading in both Put and Call *Options* for IBM, we find we have many alternatives for setting up that Hedge position.

BARRON'S

July 24, 1989

Expire date Strike price	Sales	Open Int.	Week's High	Low	Price	Net Chg.	N.Y. Close
Honwll Jul75 p	213	1392	⅛	1-16	1-16—	⅛	85½
Honwll Jul80...	5164	2204	6	1⅛	5⅛+	2½	85½
Honwll Jul80 p	1355	1102	1½	1-16	1-16—	1⅜	85½
Humana Aug35.	140	1016	2 7-16	2⅛	2⅜+	⅛	37⅛
Humana Nov30.	108	391	7½	7½	7½—	¼	37⅛
Humana Feb35	206	449	4⅛	4	4⅛+	⅜	37⅛
InfoRs Nov10..	60	65	1¼	1	1¼—3-16		10¼
I B M Aug105..	467	1331	12	8¾	9¼—	1¼	114⅜
I B M Aug105 p	772	2163	7-16	3-16	3-16—	⅛	114⅜
I B M Aug110..	7034	6048	7½	3¾	5 —	1	114⅜
I B M Aug110 p	5654	5934	2⅞	11-16	15-16—3-16		114⅜
I B M Aug115	20965	16772	3¾	1½	1 15-16—11-16		114⅜
I B M Aug115 p	5487	4193	4	¾	3⅛+	⅛	114⅜
I B M Aug120..	17480	11728	1⅜	½	⅝—7-16		114⅜
I B M Aug120 p	771	549	8⅛	5¼	7 +	⅛	114⅜
I B M Oct105..	442	5010	13½	10⅛	11⅜—	⅛	114⅜
I B M Oct105 p.	577	4770	1 1-16	¾	⅞—1-16		114⅜
I B M Oct110..	1310	5235	9⅝	6⅝	7⅜—	1⅛	114⅜
I B M Oct110 p	1958	5030	2⅝	1⅝	2 1-16...		114⅜
I B M Oct115..	5464	9946	6⅜	3¾	4½—	¾	114⅜
I B M Oct115 p	2087	6262	4⅞	3⅜	4¼+	¼	114⅜
I B M Oct120..	→		3⅞	2	2½—	½	114⅜
I B M Oct120 p	385	8890	8¾	5⅞	7¼+	⅛	114⅜
I B M Oct125...	2363	9520	2 1-16	15-16	1⅛—9-16		114⅜
I B M Oct125 p	125	283	12	10	12 +	1¼	114⅜
I B M Oct130..	1438	5708	1	7-16	9-16—	¼	114⅜
I B M Jan105 p	700	2058	1¾	1½	1¾—	⅛	114⅜
I B M Jan110..	221	983	12	9⅛	10 —	1	114⅜
I B M Jan110 p	531	929	3¾	2¾	3⅜......		114⅜
I B M Jan115..	320	2794	8⅞	6⅜	7 —	¾	114⅜
I B M Jan115 p	52	244	5¾	4⅝	5¾+	⅝	114⅜
I B M Jan120..	718	1284	6⅛	4⅜	4½—	⅞	114⅜
I B M Jan120 p	50	100	8½	7½	8½+	½	114⅜
I B M Jul105...	3485	7047	11½	7⅜	9⅛—	⅞	114⅜
I B M Jul110...	19292	12805	6¾	2½	4¼—	⅞	114⅜
I B M Jul110 p	4874	13965	⅛	1-16	1-16—1-16		114⅜
I B M Jul115.	47697	20626	2¼	1-16	1-16—1 1-16		114⅜
I B M Jul115 p.	20958	7592	2½	7-16	13-16—	⅜	114⅜
I B M Jul120..	13627	18043	7-16	1-16	1-16—3-16		114⅜
I B M Jul120 p	2514	814	7⅛	3½	6⅛+	⅝	114⅜
I B M Jul125...	879	11257	1-16	1-16	1-16......		114⅜
I B M Jul125 p	116	57	11⅞	9⅞	11⅞+	⅞	114⅜
In Flv Aug55...	172	1204	2⅞	2	2 +	¾	56¼
In Flv Aug55 p.	82	229	¾	7-16	¾—	1¼	56¼
In Flv ~~Aug60~~	400	~~202~~	¼	⅜	~~3-16~~ 2-16		56¼
In ~~Nov~~					2		¼
In Flv Jul50....	402	5	7⅛	6½	6½+	1½	56¼

246

We shall consider only one such Hedge, and we first assume that we have paid 12-1/2 for the Score, laying out $1,250. We have an arrow pointing to the October 120 Call Option in the excerpt from the Option tables as they appeared in **Barron's**. That Call Option had a high of 3-7/8, a low of 2 and a close at 2-1/2 for the week. Let us assume that we *sold short* 1 October 120 Call Option at *3*, taking in $300.

Should IBM common be selling lower than 120 in the third week in October (a decent bet), the Option will expire worthless, and we pocket the $300 we had received upon the short-sale.

Earning $300 on a $1,250 investment is a 24% return, but that was done in *3 months*, and on the basis of an *annualized return*, we would earn *96%!* In actuality, the return is even higher, because when you sell an Option short, your account is immediately credited with the proceeds, so the net investment was $1,250 minus $300, or *$950*, which would send the annualized return to considerable heights.

There are many "variations on a theme" in what we have just described. You could reduce any possible risk by a Hedge position in the ratio of Long *200* IBM Scores, Short 1 IBM Call Option, trading a lower (but still ample) return, for *much* lower loss potential.

You could also consider selling short a different Option from the point of view of its Strike Price, or its exercise month. There are many combinations which we would consider to be very attractive from the point of view of rate of return and a particular risk/return ratio.

One other point must be mentioned. In such a Hedge

position, one need not wait for the expiration day of the Call Option sold short to close out the position. At any time *during* the period that the short-sale is in operation, if time attrition and/or a decline in IBM common stock causes the Option to sell considerably lower, the profit can be taken at such time, to await another opportunity to set up a new position along the same lines.

In what we are describing, the IBM Scores can be *a long-term holding,* and we would set up a Hedge position at an advantageous time. For example, if IBM common has a couple of good days and moves up a few points, the *Call Options* would move up as well, and we would be *watching* for just such an opportunity to sell Options short at those higher levels.

Finally, if IBM developed more strength than we were looking for, the short-sale could be covered, even at some moderate loss, with the profits from previous gains with successful Hedge positions more than making up for any such loss. In other words, while some individual Hedge positions might result in losses from time to time, the *over-all* outcome would, we feel, be quite profitable.

We have just described (a) a low-risk trading strategy for the IBM Score itself, and (b) a potentially very high-yield IBM Score/Option Hedge position. What we have described is applicable to other Scores as well at the present time, and as the market fluctuates, *additional* Scores would move into positions where these approaches could be profitably followed.

There is a *whole range* of profit-promising positions that can be taken with the 26 Scores on top blue chip companies, whether for leveraged profit on the upside, as we described with the A T & T Score, or for short-term trading and Hedge positions, as we described with the IBM Score. We feel certain that close attention paid by investors to Scores will be well rewarded!

CURRENT SUPPLEMENT AVAILABLE

As this book was going to press, important developments were taking place. Long-Term *Warrants* on dozens of the most important Japanese companies, already trading in Europe, will, before too long, trade in the United States as well.

Stock Index *Futures* and Stock Index *Options* on the Japanese stock markets are already trading in Japan and elsewhere, and are preparing to trade in the United States. They will be highly-important speculative mediums, along the lines set forth in this book.

In the **Current Supplement,** the latest approaches to Index Option speculation are described, in light of the most recent stock market action.

In addition, the Current Supplement contains a valuable alphabetical listing by *Industry Group*, of all Warrants, Convertibles and Scores trading today, plus other current information important in today's market, regarding these fields.

The publishers of this book would like to send you this Current Supplement. Just send your name and address to:

Current Supplement, Department 96
R.H.M. Press
172 Forest Avenue
Glen Cove, New York 11542

There is no cost or obligation.

CONVERTIBLES

Having been Editor of the **R.H.M. Convertible Survey** since *1956*, which means 33 years of experience as we write, we are emphatically aware of the fact that few investors appreciate what can be accomplished in the securities markets with *Convertibles* — Convertible Bonds and Convertible Preferred Stocks.

The potential advantages which can accrue to knowledgeable investors are *far* greater than most professional advice (from brokers, advisers etc.) envisages.

In this section of the book, we will be bringing those very positive factors to the attention of the reader, but let us begin with definitions and a quick look at some of the most important — and most obvious! — accomplishments which Convertibles can bring to bear on one's investment results.

Defining Convertibles

Convertible Bonds and Convertible Preferred Stocks are senior securities of a company, entitled to their full interest or dividend payments before the common stock can get a cent in dividends, and having a claim on assets of the company to their full face value, ahead of the common stock.

In addition to these typical attributes of any senior security of a company, a *Convertible* Bond or *Convertible* Preferred Stock is exchangeable for a stated number of shares of common stock of the company, for a stated

251

period of time, usually 10 or 20 years, whenever the holder of the Convertible wishes to make the exchange.

Therefore, when a common stock has had a sufficient rise, the Convertible will rise as well, on conversion value, and we will shortly illustrate that. But when the common stock *falls*, the attributes of a senior security, which we described above, plus the rising *yield* of the Convertible as it sells at lower prices, causes the Convertible to first fall at a slower rate than the common stock, and then to reach a point where it virtually refuses to fall any further, even if the common stock continues to move lower.

Typically, when "well-situated," a Convertible will show *far* less downside loss, when the common is falling, yet will show just as much, or almost as much, upside appreciation, when the common stock is rising. We will shortly be demonstrating how these attributes of well-situated Convertibles are invaluable in aiming at substantial capital gains in *any* part of the market cycle.

How One "Throws Money Out The Window"
By Not Following Convertibles

Even on the simplest level, Convertibles can reward the investor who follows the rule:

"Never Buy A Common Stock —
Without First Checking To See If There Is a
Convertible Trading For The Same Company"

Thus, consider the Convertible Bonds for **Nationwide Cellular Service Inc.**, which company saw revenues grow from $5.2 million in 1985 to $30.1 million in 1987, in various aspects of the fast-growing cellular telephone industry, and being typical of the hundreds of young growth companies that have issued Convertibles in recent years.

These Convertibles trade as the "9s of '02," meaning that each $100 face value of Bond pays $9.00 in interest per annum, whatever the current market price of the Bond, and that the Bond will be paid off at full face value in 2002.

Now consider the following facts as of the **R.H.M. Convertible Survey** issue of July 15, 1988, when the statistical section showed the common stock of Nationwide Cellular Service selling at 9-5/16 (9.3125) and the Convertible 9s of '02 selling at 80-7/8 (80.875).

Each $100 face value of Bond is *convertible* into 8.696 shares of Nationwide Cellular Service common stock, any time the holder of the Bond wishes to make the exchange.

At 9-5/16, 8.696 shares had a market value of 80.9, which is almost exactly where the Convertible Bond was trading (80-7/8).

FACT: No matter how high Nationwide Cellular might go, the Convertible Bond *had* to match its gain, dollar-for-dollar invested. Thus, Nationwide Cellular doubles from 9-5/16 to 18-5/8, up 100%. Since each $100 face value of Bond continues to be convertible into (exchangeable for) 8.696 shares of common, when that common is at 18-5/8, the Bond *must* have a minimum value of 8.696 x 18.625, or 161.96. In moving from 80-7/8 to 161.96, the Bond has *also* gone up by 100%, matching the gain in the common, as it *had* to.

Any Convertible selling at "Conversion Parity" (the market price of the Convertible equal to the market value of the common shares for which, on demand, it can be exchanged) *must* show the same percentage profit as the common on any *upside* move, through "Conversion Value."

Further, by the same indisputable arithmetic, an investment in the Convertible can *not* show a greater percentage *loss* than the common stock on any downside move.

Thus, Nationwide Cellular *drops* by 50% from 9-5/16 to about 4.65. *Now*, the minimum value of the Bond is 8.696 x 4.65, which equals 40.43. From 80-7/8 to 40.43 is just about a 50% drop, equaling the common stock decline. No matter how much the common stock will decline, the Convertible Bond can *not* have a *greater* percentage decline.

(In point of fact, most Convertibles show far *less* loss than their respective common stocks on the downside, which is where we enter the area of how Convertibles can sharply improve one's stock market performance — but for that, read what follows later.)

So we are back to mid-July 1988, with Nationwide Cellular common at 9-5/16 and the Convertible 9s of '02 at 80-7/8, and each dollar invested in the Convertible Bond *must* show at least as much percentage profit as the same dollar invested in the common on the upside and can *not* show a greater percentage loss on the downside.

Before we demonstrate how well-situated Convertibles can play a superb role in aiming at stock market profits, able to minimize risk and maximize gain, let us begin by explaining this beginning point of how ignorance of Convertibles can cause an investor to *throw money, in substantial quantities, out the window!*

Assume an $8,087 investment in $10,000 face value of the Nationwide Cellular Service Convertible 9s of '02 at 80-7/8, and the same amount invested in 868 shares of Nationwide Cellular common stock at 9-5/16.

In one year's time, the investment in the Convertible Bond would earn interest of $9 per $100 face value of Bond, or $900 for the $10,000 face value of Bonds purchased.

But Nationwide Cellular common stock pays no dividend, so the return here would be 0. Annually, the investment in the Convertible Bonds *would earn $900 more* than the equal dollar investment in the common stock.

Further, Bonds have a low commission rate — about $7.50 for each $1,000 face value of Bond — so the commission on the $10,000 face value of Nationwide Cellular Bonds would be $75, or $150 on a "round trip" of buying and selling.

In contrast, buying 868 shares of Nationwide Cellular Service *common stock* at 9-5/16, would have a commission cost at the typical brokerage house of about $230, and about another $230 when one sold.

This comes to $460 for a "round trip," or $310 extra

commission when buying the common stock, as against buying the same dollar amount in the Convertible Bonds.

SIMPLE QUESTION: If, in early-July 1988, $8,087 invested in Nationwide Cellular Convertible Bonds *had* to show exactly as much percentage gain as the same amount invested in Nationwide Cellular common stock on the upside, and *could not* show any greater percentage loss than the common on the downside, and if the Convertible investment paid $900 in interest where the common paid nothing, and if the round trip commission on the Convertible investment rather than the common saved about $310 in commissions, why should *any* investor have purchased the common rather than the Convertible, when by doing so, that investor threw *$1,210* out the window, without any compensating advantage whatever?

The answer, of course, is that there is no reason whatever to throw away that $1,210, taking an immediate 15% loss. Why then do investors do this over and over again, not only with Nationwide Cellular, but with hundreds of other common/Convertible alternatives in all stages of the market cycle?

The answer here is that *very few* investors are aware of what we have just described. And even when an investor has some knowledge of what Convertibles are, the investor buying a common stock does not have the tools at hand to *check to see* if a well-situated Convertible is available as an alternative purchase.

Here is where a computerized statistical section, such as can be found weekly in the **R.H.M. Convertible Survey** performs an invaluable function. In the 18 pages of computer-generated statistical coverage of more than 900 Convertibles, the information for each Convertible is available on a separate line, telling one at a glance when a Convertible is selling at or near zero premium over Conversion Value (which is when a Convertible *must* show as much percentage profit as the common on any upside move), and what the comparative yield is for common and Convertible.

This information allows one, whenever a purchase of a common stock is being considered, to check the latest statistical information to make certain that one is not immediately throwing about 15% of one's investment "out-the-window," as we described with Nationwide Cellular Service 9s of '02.

On a separate page, we show part of a reduced (and edited) representation of the weekly statistical section from the 7-15-88 Survey issue. For space reasons, we have divided the one-line presentation into two parts, but note that the line giving the statistical information for Nationwide Cellular Service is directly above the heavy, wavy line.

To further fit the statistical excerpt on the page, the first and last columns have been dropped, the first column giving recommendations, and the last column giving numbers for the various "Footnotes" affecting individual Convertibles, which Footnotes are found elsewhere in each Survey issue.

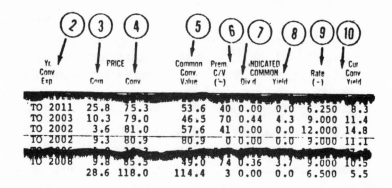

Idd Com-Cv		ISSUE		CONVERSION Price ($)	Rate (Shares)
O-O	(B)	NAC RE CORP 6.250-11		48.12	2.078
S-S	(B)	NAFCO FIN 9.000-03		22.16	4.512
A-A	(B)	NASTA INTL 12.000-02		6.25	16.000
O-O	(B)	NATIONWIDE CELL 9.000-02		11.50	8.696
S-S	(B)	NATL CONV ST 9.000-08	R	20.00	5.000
S-S	(B)	NATL EDUCAT 6.500-11	R	25.00	4.000

Yr. Conv Exp	PRICE Com	Conv	Common Conv. Value	Prem. C/V (%)	INDICATED COMMON Div d	Yield	Rate (-)	Cur Conv Yield
TO 2011	25.8	75.3	53.6	40	0.00	0.0	6.250	8.3
TO 2003	10.3	79.0	46.5	70	0.44	4.3	9.000	11.4
TO 2002	3.6	81.0	57.6	41	0.00	0.0	12.000	14.8
TO 2002	9.3	80.9	80.9	0	0.00	0.0	9.000	11.1
TO 2008	9.8	85.5	49.0	74	0.36	3.7	9.000	10.5
	28.6	118.0	114.4	3	0.00	0.0	6.500	5.5

The first few columns are self-explanatory, telling where common and Convertible are traded, the name of the Convertible, including the rate of annual interest or dividend, and the maturity date where there is a Bond involved.

The column headed by (1), the *"Conversion Rate,"* gives a most significant figure, the number of shares of common stock into which each $100 face value of Bond, or each share of Preferred, can be converted. Column (2) gives the year the Conversion privilege expires. Column (3) and (4) respectively, give the current price of the common stock and the Convertible.

When these new prices are inserted each week, the computer multiplies Column (1), the Conversion Rate, by Column (3), the common price, and we get the *Conversion Value*, which is Column (5). The computer then divides the Conversion Value into the current price of the Bond, or the Preferred Stock (4), and comes up with the *Premium Over Conversion Value*, which is Column (6).

Moving over to Column (8), the current *Yield* on the common stock is computed by dividing the common stock price, Column (3), into the annual dividend paid on the common, which is given in column (7). The current *Yield* on the Convertible (10), is computed by dividing the Convertible price, Column (4), into the interest or dividend rate of the Convertible, Column (9).

The remarkable usefulness of a weekly statistical presentation now becomes very clear by looking at the excerpt shown, the arrow pointing to **Nationwide Cell(ular) 9.000-02**. The premium over Conversion

Value (6) is *zero*, so we know the Convertible *must* show the same percentage rise as the common stock on any advance, and can *not* show any greater percentage loss on the downside.

Then we move over to the right and find the common pays no dividend (8), so there is a zero yield, while the then current yield on the Convertible (10) is *11.1%*. On the basis of what we have just described, the statistical table would tell us that it is *utter foolishness* to buy the common stock of Nationwide Cellular when the well-situated Convertible is available.

We now come to:

The Most IMPORTANT Attribute Of A Convertible

Thus far we have demonstrated that at Conversion Parity (the Convertible selling at a price equal to the market value of the common stock for which it can be exchanged), the Convertible *must* show as much percentage gain as the common stock on the upside, and can *not* show any greater percentage loss on the downside.

But, while the Convertible cannot show a *greater* percentage decline than the common stock, there is no compulsion to show *as* great a decline. And the fact is that most Convertibles show less percentage loss on the downside, many times *far* less.

We can illustrate this with the actual previous market action of Nationwide Cellular Convertible Bonds. In the Survey issue of 1-1-88, the stock market was at a much lower point, and Nationwide Cellular common stock was selling at 4. At that price, with each $100 face value of Bond, remember, convertible into 8.696 shares of Nationwide Cellular common, the Conversion Value of the Bond was 4 x 8.696, or *34.78.*

If the Convertible had actually *fallen* to 34.78, it would have shown *as great* a percentage loss as the common, but *no greater.* (By definition, a Convertible cannot fall below its Conversion Value.) But the Nationwide Cellular Convertible Bonds did not fall as low as 34.78. Instead, they sold no lower than *63.*

Why did Nationwide Cellular Convertible Bonds refuse to decline as much as the common stock? To begin with, throughout our more than three decades of analyzing Convertibles, virtually *all* Convertibles have held up better than their common stocks, when those common stocks went into noticeable decline.

First there is the typically *higher yield.* At 63 for the Convertible 9s of 2002, the yield was *14.29%*, while the common had a 0 yield, and any additional decline by the Convertible would have boosted the Convertible yield still further, so the rising yield acted as a strong brake against further decline.

Secondly, and even more important, there was the very long-term *conversion privilege* into the common stock. Each $100 face value of Bond could be converted into 8.696 shares of Nationwide Cellular common stock until the year 2002.

We know very well from the Option market that even a *3-month* "Call" on a popular stock has a substantial market value. A *14-year* "Call" on a common stock has a *very* large value, and as the Convertible declines in price, this valuable "Call" privilege becomes available at a lower and lower price, acting as the most important brake on the decline in the Convertible.

Considering Convertibles as a group, as *senior securities of the company*, there is also the right of the Convertible to receive its full Bond interest or Preferred dividend payments before the common stock could get any dividends at all, and a prior claim to assets ahead of the common stock.

All these factors combine to buttress the Convertible price during a common stock decline. To fully appreciate the *large* advantage of the well-situated Convertible in protecting investors against downside risk to a *far* greater degree than the respective common stock, let us go back to our two alternative investments of $8,087 in $10,000 face value of Nationwide Cellular 9s of 2002 at 80-7/8, and the same $8,087 invested in 868 shares of Nationwide Cellular common stock at 9-5/16.

Taking the early-January prices of 4 for the common stock and 63 for the Convertible Bond (typically, in a decline, they would react back approximately to the same levels), a retreat back to those lows would have produced the following comparative losses:

In falling from 80-7/8 to 63,
the $8,087 invested in the Nationwide
Cellular *Convertible Bonds*
would have lost 17-7/8 points on
$10,000 face value of Bonds,
for a loss of *$1,787*

In falling from 9-5/16 to 4, the
$8,087 invested in Nationwide Cel-
lular *common stock* would have
lost 5-5/16 points on 868 shares
for a loss of *$4,611*

On the downside, Nationwide Cellular Convertible Bonds would show a *far* smaller loss than Nationwide Cellular common stock.

It is clear, then, that the investor in mid-July 1988 who was not aware of the availability of the Nationwide Cellular Convertible Bond, and, therefore, purchased the common stock, *not only* threw $900 in Bond interest out the window, and paid about $310 more in brokerage commissions than necessary, *but also opened himself up to the far greater downside risks in Nationwide Cellular common.* ALL these large disadvantages were embraced to no purpose whatever, because of simple lack of knowledge of what Convertibles are, and what they can accomplish.

Attractive Convertibles At Premiums
OVER Conversion Value

Explaining the superior performance of well-situated Convertibles with **Nationwide Cellular** as an example, now needs to be broadened, because while that Convertible was selling at 0 premium over Conversion Value, making for very simple calculations, this does *not* mean that a Convertible selling at a premium *over* Conversion Value cannot be similarly superior. Far from it!

In essence, the premium in such circumstances, is *one of the costs involved* in securing for ourselves the benefits of a well-situated Convertible, which can still reward an investor in exactly the same manner as it was described with Nationwide Cellular.

To demonstrate that the benefits gained can far outweigh the "cost" of the premium, let us look at the action of a Convertible which performed very well in mid-1988.

In the **R.H.M. Convertible Survey** of 6-17-88, the common stock of **International Game Technology,** a $100 million-in-revenues world leader in the development of microprocessor-based gaming products, was selling at *15-3/8*, while the company's Convertible *7-3/4s of 2002* were selling at *114*.

With each $100 face value of Bond convertible into 6.78 shares of common stock, the Conversion Value was 15.375 x 6.78, which equals *104.24.* Since the Convertible Bond was selling at *114*, the computer on that date, divided 114 by 104.24 and came up with a premium over Conversion Value of *9%*. That premium did not in the least dissuade us from continuing to recommend this Convertible as a "Buy."

We now go to early-August, and find that International Game Technology common stock has moved ahead strongly, from the 15-3/8 level that had obtained on June 17, to 24-1/2. At that price, the Convertible was worth 24.50 x 6.78 on straight Conversion Value, or 166-1/8, and that is where the Convertible sold.

The common stock had advanced *59%*, while the Convertible Bond had advanced *46%*. Would an investor have been better off on June 17 buying the common stock at 15-3/8 rather than the Convertible Bond at 114, since the gain had been greater for the common?

The answer is strongly in the negative. The moderately higher profit for the common as against the Convertible was *far* from compensating for (a) the 6.8% yield for the Convertible against the 0 yield for the common, (b) the much higher commission rate in buying the common rather than the Convertible, and, most important (c) the much greater downside safety for capital represented by the Convertible.

To demonstrate the latter point, we go back to the 1-29-88 issue of the **R.H.M. Convertible Survey,** where we find International Game Technology common stock at *9-1/8* and the Convertible 7-3/4s of 2002 selling at *90*.

As with Nationwide Cellular, we go back to the prices obtaining in the Survey of 6-17-88 and assume two alternative investments:

(1) An $11,400 investment in $10,000 face value of the International Game Technology 7-3/4s of 2002 at 114; and

(2) The same $11,400 investment in 741 shares of International Game Technology common stock at 15-3/8.

With the experience-justified assumption that if the common stock dropped back to its 1-29-88 price of *9-1/8*, the Convertible would hold at *its* 1-29-88 level of *90*, the following comparative losses would have ensued:

> In falling from 114 to 90, the
> $11,400 invested in the International
> Game Technology *Convertible Bonds*
> would have lost 24 points on $10,000
> face value of Bonds for a loss of *$2,400*

> In falling from 15-3/8 to 9-1/8, the
> $11,400 invested in International
> Game Technology *common stock*
> would have lost 6-1/4 points on
> 741 shares for a loss of *$4,631*

Once again, the percentage loss for the common would have been *far* greater than what would have been suffered by the Convertible Bonds.

And we must not forget that the moderately higher percentage profit with the common stock in the upside run, due to the premium, was offset to a considerable degree by the much higher commission costs in buying the common stock, and the yield on the Convertible which, if the position was held for some time, as is true of most positions, soon becomes significant.

As a point of *great importance*, let us explain the following: *because* the downside protection was so substantial, compared with the risky common stock, it would have been well justified, and prudent, to take a *considerably larger position* in the Convertible Bonds of International Game Technology in June 1988 than would have been true with the common stock, and the result of the subsequent run-up in the common would have been a *far* larger dollar profit with the Convertible position, quickly wiping out the small profit advantage in the common stock, and then going far beyond it in ultimate profits with the Convertible.

A premium over Conversion Value in no way negates the *large* advantage of a "well-situated" Convertible!

Having established this point, it is clear that hundreds of attractive Convertible opportunities are available for the knowledgeable investor who knows how to *follow* Convertibles, and how to *use* them.

Deep-Discount Convertibles

The long list of opportunities in this sector of Convertibles is best understood by asking yourself a question: "What if I could make an investment where downside risk was very small, the yield ranged from good-to-excellent, and there was every prospect for expecting later capital gains of *large* dimensions?'' We would hardly expect your answer to that question to be anything but: "Let's make those investments!''

Yet, just as with investors who invest in the *common stock* of a company, rather than with a well-situated *Convertible* for the same company, by which action they typically throw about 12% to 15% of the money invested out-the-window, and embrace much greater downside risk to their capital, all with no compensating advantages whatever, it is *lack of knowledge* that causes investors to miss the Convertible opportunities with the outstanding investment characteristics we have just described.

What must be kept in mind is that dozens of new Convertibles are being issued in any given, say, six-month period, and once the Convertible is issued, it is a *contract* between the holder of the Convertible and the company that issued it. (All this applies to the more than 900 Convertibles currently trading, as well.)

The company has promised to pay a stated interest on the face value of the Convertible, if it is a Convertible Bond, or a stated dividend per share of Convertible Preferred Stock, and has also guaranteed that any time the holder of the Convertible wishes to do so, the Convertible can be exchanged for a certain number of shares of common stock.

Following the issuance of the Convertible, some unfortunate things can happen to the company and its common stock.

The general market itself may suffer an over-all decline of some dimensions. The *Group* with which the common stock is associated may fall into investor disfavor. There may be a few quarters where earnings are disappointing to security analysts, whose opinions are widely followed.

With *any* of the above negative developments, the common stock of the company can show a considerable decline, while the *Convertible*, even if it holds up much better than the common stock on a percentage basis, can still slip well below par (100), and become a Deep-Discount Convertible.

This can create a Convertible opportunity of large dimensions. As the Convertible declined, the *yield* went higher, and soon the Convertible reached a point where it refused to decline appreciably further, even if the common stock continued to drift lower.

If analysis shows that the *longer*-term outlook for the company is still excellent, this Convertible opportunity would provide (a) a fine yield, (b) very small further downside risk, and (c) for the patient holder, excellent potential for appreciation.

United Healthcare Convertible Bonds

A Convertible we recommended for purchase in the pages of the **R.H.M Convertible Survey** has some important guideposts to illuminate in different areas of "Opportunities In Convertibles."

The first thing to emphasize is that a Convertible provides us with a *choice*, where we can set the attributes of the common stock alongside those of the Convertible, and *very often* find that the Convertible is much more promising as the purchase of choice.

Thus, with the United Healthcare 7.500-11, we pointed out in our original recommendation that the Convertible had much less *downside risk*. In the Survey of *9-30-88*, United Healthcare common had been at 4-1/4 and the Convertible at a lowly 68-1/2. (Deep-Discount, remember!)

Jumping to where we were recommending purchase, in the Survey of 4-28-89, the common stock had improved to *7-1/8*, while the Convertible had improved to *82*. If, after purchase, the market and/or the common stock had a sinking spell and common and Convertible of United Healthcare returned to their lower 9-30-88 prices, there would be a 13-1/2-point loss for the Convertible (from 82 to 68.50), representing a loss of *16.5%*. But the loss for the common would be much greater (7-1/8 to 4-1/4) representing a loss of *40.4%*.

A loss of 16.5% against a loss of 40.4%, and there is no doubt in *that* measuring tool as to whether the Convertible would be a better holding than the common. Are there other aspects to consider which would mark the common as superior to the Convertible Bond? Well, there is the 23% premium over Conversion Value that obtained for the Bond, meaning that the common stock would experience a moderately greater gain than the Convertible on any upside move. However, it would not be *much* greater, and offsetting that would be the 9.1% yield for the Convertible, when we made the recommendation, against a *0* yield for the common stock, which paid no dividend.

Also to be considered would be the fact that *commissions* to buy and to sell the common stock are much greater than would be applicable to the Convertible Bond.

Looking now at some *fundamentals* which went into this Convertible recommendation, to emphasize the importance of first deciding whether you like the company to begin with (!), United Healthcare owns and manages health maintenance organizations (HMOs), and as of year-end 1987, 34 HMOs were owned or managed in 23 states, servicing 1.5 million members.

In recent years, revenues had expanded at a rapid rate, from $14.6 million in 1983 to $101.3 million in 1985 and $440 million in 1986 (quite an advance for revenues). Earnings had difficulties keeping up with all that expansion, and then nosedived in 1987, with a loss of ($0.99) per share, followed by a steeper loss for 1988 at ($2.29) per share.

The expected happened where United Healthcare

common stock was concerned, which hit the toboggan slide!

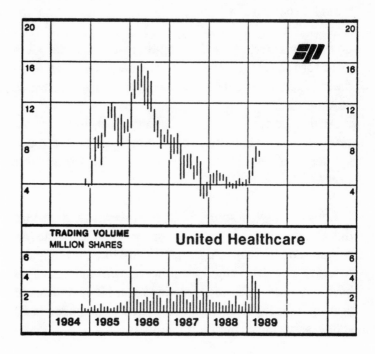

The long-term price chart (courtesy of **Standard & Poor's**) shows the steep dive, 1986 - 1987, then a sideways path during 1988, and a definitive recovery move in 1989, which has taken the common stock to the *11* mark, as of this writing.

The more favorable factors that have developed in the past 12 months have been a better environment for

Health Maintenance Organizations as a whole, a comprehensive restructuring for the company, and a new top management team, poised to start sending earnings to the upside. This should start in 1989 when analysts are looking for $0.50 per share in the black.

One of the most positive factors is firm pricing on an industry-wide basis, with such increases running between 20% to 25%. Meanwhile, the costs associated with rapid expansion in previous years, have almost all been absorbed by now, and the factors just outlined should flow directly to increased earnings.

The above has outlined the type of research into fundamentals that must become a part of any understanding of the Convertible "arithmetic" which is involved. Another important element which we now emphasize is that United Healthcare *is a low-price stock*. As such, because the Convertible Bond is necessarily *high*-priced, while the common stock is *low*-priced, each $100 face value of Convertible is exchangeable for a large number of shares (9.412 in this case), and it takes but a moderate move in the common stock to produce a *large* move in the Convertible.

This, indeed, is what happened with United Healthcare, so that in the **R.H.M. Convertible Survey** of 7-21-89, the common stock has appreciated to *11* and the Convertible 7.500-11 to *105.3*. That is now almost direct "Conversion Parity," which means that the Convertible is selling at a price almost equal to the market value of the number of shares for which it can be exchanged.

This means that the Convertible 7.500-11 will advance just as much as the common stock on a percentage basis, *if* the common stock moves *up*.

On the other hand, if the common stock and/or the stock market hit an air pocket to the downside, we would expect the Convertible to begin developing a *premium* over Conversion Value, meaning that it would have a smaller decline than the common stock on a percentage basis.

Since there is still the better-than-7%-yield for the Convertible at this level, while the common stock pays no dividend, anyone interested in taking a new position in United Healthcare should, *most distinctly* do it through the Convertible and not the common stock.

For in addition to the yield advantage, there is the large saving in commission costs, and still the downside protection for capital via the Convertible rather than the common.

This last point applies to *many* Convertible/common alternatives. If there is a negligible-to-0 premium over Conversion Value, the Convertible is almost always the better "Buy" — very often by *far* the better "Buy."

So the United Healthcare Convertible 7.500-11 have taught us how important it is to analyze the fundamentals of the company, to look for an undervalued situation where the Convertible will provide a favorable alternative to the common stock from *many* vantage points.

Another lesson has been the leverage for the Convertible when it is a Call on a low-price stock. That is, the low-price stock tends to move in big jumps on a percentage basis, and this is immediately reflected in the Convertible.

And, finally, we have seen that when the premium over Conversion Value heads towards the 0 level, the Convertible becomes very much the holding of choice, as against the common stock, if one wishes to make an investment in that situation.

The Convertible Hedge

What we have just described with United Healthcare constitutes a fine vehicle for another Convertible approach which holds excellent promise.

If the 7.500-11 are currently near 0 premium over Conversion Value because of the considerable rise in common and Convertible, and if we would expect the premium to reappear if United Healthcare now proceeded to have a relapse in the stock market, what would be the effect if we set up a *Full-Hedge*, buying X amount of Convertible, and selling short the entire amount of common stock for which the Convertible can be exchanged?

The answer is very simple. A net profit would develop which would be equal to the premium over Conversion Value that would come into being.

Let us look at the example of United Healthcare near current levels. Let us say that the common stock is selling at 11-1/4, and the Convertible 7.500-11 are selling at 105-7/8.

275

Since each $100 face value of Bond is convertible into 9.412 shares of common stock, the *Conversion Value* is 9.412 x 11.25, which comes to *105.88*. Since the Convertible is *selling* at 105-7/8, this is direct Conversion Parity.

If we now set up a position where we are Long $10,000 face value of Bond, which costs us $10,587, and Short 941 shares of common stock at 11-1/4 (which comes to about the same figure), we *know* that if the common stock moves *higher*, no net loss can develop; the Convertible must move up with the common stock, dollar-for-dollar invested.

But if the common stock moves *lower*, nothing compels the Convertible Bond to move down at the same rate as the common stock. Suppose there was a retreat back to the lows we mentioned in previous paragraphs, of 68-1/2 for the Convertible Bond and 4-1/4 for the common stock.

The Convertible, in dropping from 105-7/8 to 68-1/2 would lose 37-3/8 points, or *$3,737*.

The common stock, in dropping from 11-1/4 to 4-1/4, would lose 7 points. On the 941 shares of common stock sold short at 11-1/4, that would be a profit of 941 x 7, or *$6,587*.

Gain of $6,587, loss of $3,737, and we have a *net gain* of *$2,850*.

For different positions, the net gain would vary, depending on how much of a decline was experienced by the common stock, but there could *never* be a loss, whether United Healthcare common went up or went down!

When you establish a Full-Hedge position with a Convertible, no funds are required to carry the short-sale of the common, so whatever is earned is on the funds carrying the Convertible, and the net profit can be appreciable.

This is particularly so when there is a good-to-high yield for the Convertible, and the common is a low-price stock, subject to typically high fluctuations.

One other point should be mentioned here, regarding any Full-Hedge set up at 0 premium over Conversion Value. This is equivalent to what we call "locking in the yield," and is naturally attractive when there is that "good-to-high-yield" for the Convertible, and the common pays no dividend.

Since there can *not* be any loss in this position, in *either* direction for the common stock, the yield on the Convertible is being earned at 0 risk, which makes it equivalent to the highest-rate bond investment, *if* the company enjoys a financial position which obviates any possibility of bankruptcy, or financial stringency that might threaten interest payments. But *many* companies whose Convertibles get into this position have fine Balance Sheets.

The Half-Hedge

This position involves being Long X amount of Convertible, and Short 1/2 X the number of common shares for which the Convertible position can be exchanged.

This is a position that is bullish for the common stock, for if the common stock advances, one is, in effect, Long 1/2 the common stock holding on a net basis. This is so because our Long position in the Convertible is equivalent to *twice* the amount of common stock in the short position.

On the other hand, if the common stock disappoints us and moves *lower*, the partial short position in the common stock is enough to cover most or all of the net loss that might develop.

All this adds up to the strong advisability of watching for Convertibles that are selling at 0, or near 0, premium over Conversion Value. We can aim at very low-risk profits in *many* ways, when such obtains, and in these pages we have covered only *some* of those ways.

More On High-Yield Convertibles

There are times when excessive pessimism evidences itself for a company that has a Convertible trading, the common stock of the company declines sharply, and *because* of that "excessive" pessimism, the Convertible sells down to a price that is considerably below where it would otherwise have stabilized.

Since, quite often, such companies are "secondary" companies to begin with, their Convertibles start life with a high coupon (high interest rate), and when that Convertible sells down unduly, the yield gets into the area of what we call "High-Yield," and the Convertible typically sells at a "Deep-Discount" from par, or 100, in the case of a Convertible Bond.

Obviously, there are times when a Convertible fully deserves to sell at that deep a discount, because the excessive pessimism as to the future of the company that issued the Convertible is *justified*.

But over the years we have found that there are also many occasions when the pessimism is greatly overdone, and the Deep-Discount, High-Yield Convertible becomes a fine opportunity along a number of lines we shall now spell out.

When analyzing the merits of a Deep-Discount Convertible, the Number One question is always: will the company continue to pay the stated interest on its Convertible Bond, or the stated dividend on its Convertible Preferred Stock?

If a close examination of the company's financial condition finds no cause for worry about the ability to pay,

279

then one simply buys the High-Yield Convertible and enjoys the yield!

Barris Industries Convertibles

Barris Industries 6.750-12 were one of those Convertibles that found their way to the weekly "Recommended High Yield Convertibles" list of the **R.H.M. Convertible Survey.**

In the Survey issue of 1-6-89, the common stock was at 7.0, the Convertible down to a lowly 50.5, and selling at a 61% premium over Conversion Value.

The common paid no dividend, but at a price of 50.5, the Convertible 6.750-12 were yielding *13.4%*. When we checked out the Balance Sheet, and other relevant aspects of the company's operations, we found no cause for worry — quite the opposite — so the Convertible became a High-Yield recommendation.

Barris Industries has been, and continues to be, a success story in the creation, development and production of game shows primarily, but also some theatrical films and some additional forms of television programming.

Chuck Barris built Barris Industries, producing such popular shows as "The Newlywed Game," "The Dating Game," and "The Gong Show." Seeing no reason to change a winning formula, there followed "The New Newlywed Game" and "The All New Dating Game."

Barris not only got licensing fees from the television stations showing these programs, but also retained two 30-second spots of commercial advertising time for sale or barter. Valuable as well were about 2,500 hours of programming of the shows just mentioned, which have residual value now, and may have much more value in the future.

In December 1986, GIANT GROUP LTD. acquired about 22.5% of the company's common stock from Charles H. Barris, founder of the company, along with the right to vote additional stock owned by Barris.

Burt Sugarman, CEO of GIANT became CEO of Barris Industries and there then began a series of ambitious projects, including a failed (and expensive) attempt to take over Media General, the purchase of a paper mill, and other ventures.

Not too many in the financial community were happy with this drastic change in direction for Barris and, as seen on the price chart on the next page (courtesy of **Standard & Poor's**), the common stock had a sharp slide from a 1986 top of 28-3/4 to a low of 4-3/8 in 1987.

We did not hesitate to recommend purchase of the Convertible 6.750-12 as a "High-Yield Buy" after studying the *Balance Sheet* of the company. This is something every reader should do when considering *any* purchase of a security, and while the latest Annual Report is preferable, the latest Standard & Poor's stock report is almost always available from one's broker, and it gives the salient information.

Thus, as of the Balance Sheet dated May 31, 1988, we

look first at "Current Liabilities," which tells us what the company *owes*, and then at "Current Assets,"

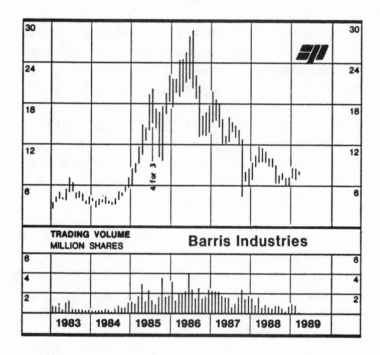

which basically is Cash, Accounts Receivable and Inventories.

In this case, *Cash* amounted to *$110 million*, which was almost triple total Current Liabilities of $41.3 million. (This was fortunate because it is not wise to take Accounts Receivable and Inventories at their stated value.)

Following this, one must look at Long-Term Debt,

and when such debt will come due for redemption. In the case of Barris Industries, virtually the only such debt was about $59 million, almost all of which was in Convertible Debentures (the one we favored buying as a High-Yield Convertible), which did not have to be paid off before *2012*, except for payments commencing in *1999* to retire the debt on an annual basis.

This was a solid financial condition, so we recommended purchase as a High-Yield Convertible, and subscribers began to enjoy that 13.4% yield.

Recognizing the values in Barris Industries, Australian financial interests stepped in to buy Mr. Sugarman's controlling interest for $34.5 million. This worked out to about $13 per share, well in excess of the then price for Barris common stock, and with this expression of confidence, the stock began to move up in the over-the-counter market, and *so did the Convertible,* not seeming so dangerous now that the Sugarman hand was off the helm of the company.

The fine Balance Sheet began to impress more analysts, and as of the July 28, 1989 issue of the **R.H.M Convertible Survey**, the 6.750-12 were selling at 67.3, *33% higher* than the 50.5 price at which the Convertible had entered our "High-Yield" list.

Once again, what we have recounted for Barris Industries Convertibles as a "High-Yield" recommendation, illustrates the many and varied Convertible opportunities that show up in the more than 900 Convertibles trading in today's market.

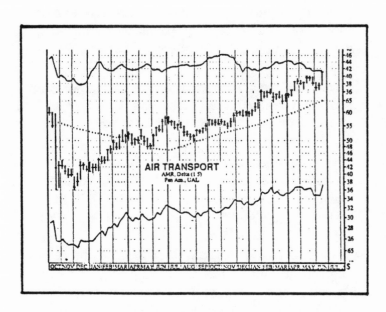

Group Movement And Convertibles

"Group Movement" — the strong tendency of stocks of companies in the same industry Group to be strong at the same time, and weak at the same time — is one part of "Technical Analysis," which deserves a *lot* of attention.

For example, look at the two Group charts (courtesy

of **Securities Research**) and ask yourself which Group you would want your investments to be in! In the Auto

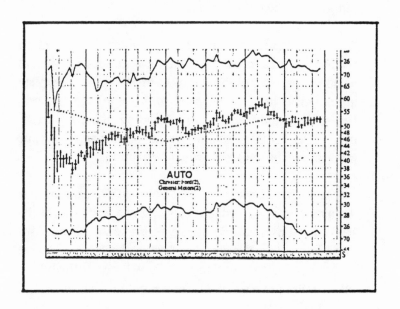

Group, every stock in the Group has turned in a dismal performance in a strong market.

This is shown as well by the *Relative Strength* line at the bottom of each chart, which shows how the Group is doing in relation to the S & P 500 Stock Index. Since the turn of the year, the Relative Strength line of the Auto Group has been continuously on the downside.

It is a totally different picture where the Air Transport (Airline) Group is concerned. Here, since December 1987, the Group has been on the upswing, and its Relative Strength line shows it to have been leading the market for the entire time.

In the "Current Supplement" which is offered to readers of this book (see the few notices of this in various parts of the book) there is a complete alphabetical breakdown by *Group* of all the Convertibles, Warrants and Scores trading in the current market, and it is a very important tool for steering your investments in the most fruitful directions.

The charts shown of the Group Movement of Air Transport and Auto stocks came from a write-up for the **R.H.M. Convertible Survey,** where a newly-issued Convertible — the **Alaska Air Group 6.875-14** — were recommended for purchase, and it will be worthwhile to take some time to look at that recommendation.

Alaska Air Group has Alaska Airlines as its chief asset, that growing passenger carrier connecting Alaska with the "lower 48," with heavy emphasis on the West Coast, but joining with American Airlines for runs into Texas, Chicago and Washington D.C. A new growth factor is taking shape through service to an increasing number of cities in Mexico.

A wholly-owned subsidiary, Horizon Air Industries, connects many small cities in western States with Alaska

Airlines' hubs.

Record earnings of about $3.15 per share are expected for 1989, with analysts looking for $3.60 per share in the

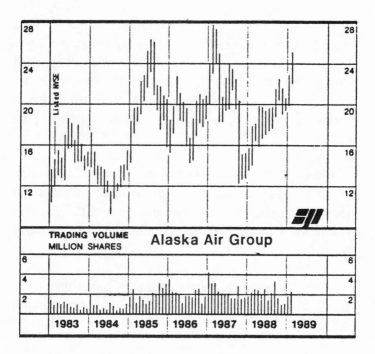

TRADING VOLUME
MILLION SHARES   Alaska Air Group

1983 1984 1985 1986 1987 1988 1989

following year.

The climb in book value from $10.12 per share in 1984 to $14.31 per share in 1986 and $19.95 per share in 1988, with a large jump to an estimated $28 per share in 1990, emphasizes the underlying strength of company activities, and it all adds up to a very favorable outlook.

There has also been quite a bit of realistic talk about possible acquisition plans by various financial interests, and if this eventuated, it would undoubtedly be at a considerably higher price than the 27-1/4 level as we write.

The price chart of Alaska Air Group on the previous page (courtesy of **Standard & Poor's**) shows the stock breaking through a "Triple Top" when it pushed through to the 30 mark, and given the strong Group chart, and the growth outlook for Alaska Airlines itself, the new Convertible, as we saw it, distinctly merited purchase.

Although there is a 27% premium over Conversion Value in effect as we write, to our mind this is much more than offset by what we would expect to be *strong resistance to decline* in the event that the common stock moved to the downside.

Then there is the 6.7% yield for the Convertible, compared with the miniscule 0.7% yield for the common stock.

And, affecting our feelings about this Convertible, is the *strong Group chart*, which increases the chances for additional forward movement in the common stock, which will begin to move the Convertible to higher levels.

Readers should learn to pay careful attention to "Group Movement" in *every* phase of their investment activities!

How A Well-Situated Convertible Can Turn
A Speculation Into An Investment

Trading over-the-counter, **Lyphomed** common stock has experienced a number of ups and downs, and was

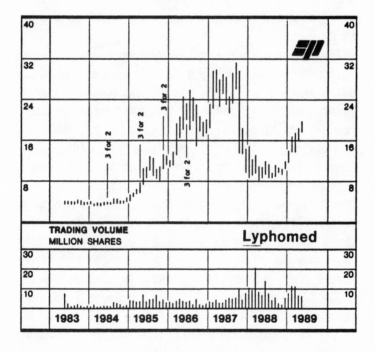

well into one of its "downs," when news came of approval by the Federal Drug Administration for the com-

289

pany's experimental aerosol form of pentamidine to treat AIDS-related pneumonia. With a potentially huge market for this drug, speculators boomed Lyphomed stock, as can be seen on the chart on the previous page (courtesy of **Standard & Poor's**), running the stock from about 8 to 20.

The company had considerable potential throughout its main business of producing and supplying intravenous pharmaceutical products, which are used in nutritional and therapeutic support of critical care patients.

Earnings had been moving along very nicely — $0.16 per share in 1984, $0.54 per share in 1986 and $0.70 per share in 1987 — when one of the company's main plants received a regulatory reprimand from the FDA, resulting in expensive product recalls.

The result was a ($0.70) per share loss in 1988, and a deep dive in the common stock from 31-1/4 to 8-1/8, part of that decline being the 1987 market crash itself. But the recall problem is now well behind the company, with revenues growing again, a number of proprietary drugs having large potential, and the speculative excitement over the AIDS-related drug, and at this point there enters the company's *Convertible Bonds* — the *5.500-12*, — selling at 69-1/2 as we write, with the common selling at 19-1/8.

The most important point to look at here is *downside protection* for the Convertible, as against the common stock, in view of the speculative nature of the company's operations.

In the Survey issue of January 6, 1989, we find

Lyphomed common stock at 11-1/2 and the Convertible 5.500-12 at 56.00. To demonstrate how much downside protection there is for the Convertible at current levels, assume an investment in $10,000 face value of the bonds at 69-1/2, at a cost of *$6,950*. Now consider an alternate investment in 363 shares of the common stock at its current price of 19-1/8, which comes to $6,942, the cost being about equal to that for the Convertible.

If the common stock should decline back to that January 1989 low of 11-1/2, there would be a 7-5/8-point loss on 363 shares, which comes to a loss of *$2,768*. In contrast, if the Convertible also declined back to its January 1989 price of 56.00 (which we would expect to approximately happen) there would be a 13-1/2-point loss on $10,000 face value of bond, which comes to a loss of *$1,350*.

$2,768 loss for the same dollar investment in the common, as against a loss in the same period of time of only *$1,350* for the Convertible, and the superior downside protection of the Convertible at current levels is very clear. Then, of course, there is also the *7.9%* yield for the Convertible, against a 0 yield for the common stock.

If one wishes to take a position in the future of Lyphomed, the Convertible 5.500-12 are *by far* the better choice.

And this, once again, makes very emphatic, the need for *every* investor to always be aware of a possible Convertible alternative investment, when one wishes to buy *any* common stock!

Pyramiding With Index Options

It is entirely fitting that we should end this book with a review of what is without question the most potentially rewarding speculative approach to the stock market that one could imagine.

This does not mean that Warrants and Convertibles do not play very important roles in building capital, as we have described in some depth in the previous chapters. But, if handled correctly, Pyramiding With Index Options has such enormous potential, that we cannot see any intelligent approach to the stock market failing to understand and fully utilize this fascinating approach to market profits.

Let us review the series of 1985 events where, in the weekly issues of the **R.H.M. Survey,** we followed a step-by-step process which resulted in an investment of $937 becoming worth $495,125 in little more than two months time.

This was a two-step Pyramid in 1985 in which the November 265 Call Options, and the December 275 Call Options for the Major Market Index, were the two "players."

The first issue in which we drew the attention of subscribers to the November 265 Call Option was dated September 27, 1985. We began by discussing the S & P 100 Index, about which we said: "November is the near-month, and the 185 Striking Price is about right for the Call Option . . . "

A few sentences later, we said: "For the Major Market Index, that Index is at *251.81*, and the correct Options are the November 260 and 265 *Calls* . . . " (Original emphasis.)

All Index Option speculation must follow Trend Line Analysis carefully, because of the invaluable clues that flow from that part of "Technical Analysis."

Special Note: This is an important analysis, and we will be trying, wherever possible to have the text that is discussing a chart or table to be on the same page, or an adjacent page, so that the reader does not have to turn a page back and forth to follow the reasoning. To accomplish this, we will be leaving some "white space" wherever necessary.

In this case, an *important* clue came in the Survey issue of 10-18-85 when we presented the chart shown of the NYSE Market Index (courtesy of the **New York Times**).

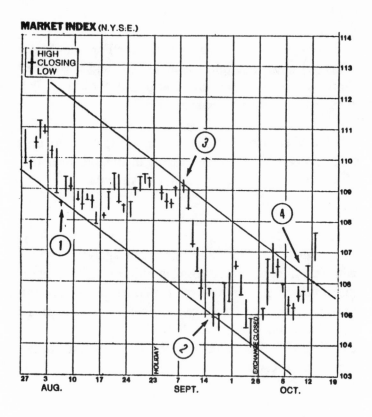

The bullish prognosis for an *upside breakout*, from what had been a *descending Trend Channel* should be clear, even to those not familiar with this type of analysis. (1), (2) and (3) define the Trend Channel, while (4) points to the breakout, with its bullish portents. From the evidence of that chart, we stated in that same Survey issue of 10-18-85 that: "Now, of course, the emphasis shifts to *Call* Index Options . . . " (Original emphasis.)

In the Survey of 11-22-85, we presented an updated chart of the NYSE Market Index (courtesy of the **New York Times** — unavoidably, it is on the next page), which well illustrated that the original upside breakout noted had moved further in the same direction (up), and had proceeded to create *another uptrend Channel*, ensuring the success of the Pyramiding, which we described as follows in the Survey issue of 11-29-85:

"In this case, anyone watching the different out of the money Index Options (*which we have been advising doing on a daily basis*), would have seen that the original speculation in November 265 Call Options had advanced from 3/16 to 7/8, a $937.50 investment having become worth *$4,475.00*, and that another Call Index Option had moved into position — the December 275 Call Option, *also* selling at 3/16. To get *powerful leverage*, you switch from the first commitment at 3/16, only now, with the profits from the first speculation, you can buy *233* of the December 275 Call Index Options at 3/16." (Original emphasis throughout.)

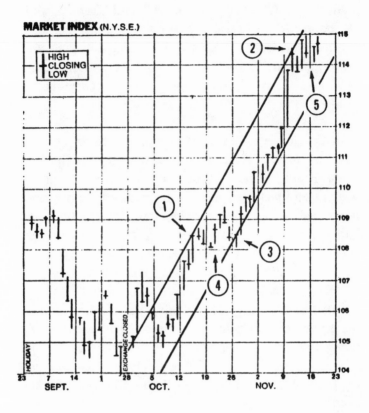

The table on the next page is taken from the 12-6-85 issue of the **R.H.M. Survey,** where we reviewed the steps of the successful Pyramid, and those steps were (1) the initial purchase of 50 November 265 Call Options for $937.50; (2) the taking of profits at (2), where the November 265 Call Options were sold at 7/8, taking in $4,475.00, and (3) the *pyramiding* of that amount into 233 December 275 Call Options when selling at 3/16.

1985	XMI	Change	November 265	November 260	December 265	December 270	December 275	December 280	December 285
9-24	251.81	-2.20	3/8	1-1/8	1-1/4				
9-25	251.59	-0.22	3/16	5/8	5/8				
9-26	249.97	+1.62	3/16	5/8	5/8				
9-30	250.39	+0.42	3/16	9/16	9/16				
10-1	253.96	+3.57	3/8	1-1/8	1				
10-2	251.72	-2.24	1/4	13/16	11/16				
10-3	251.64	-0.08	3/16	13/16	11/16				
10-4	25⌀	-1.36	3/16	9/16	1/2				
10-7	2⌀ ①		3/16	5/8	5/8				
10-8	25⌀	+0.45	3/16	5/8	5/8				
10-9	250.79	+0.12	3/16	9/16	9/16				
10-10	250.73	-0.06	3/16	5/8	9/16				
10-11	252.71	+1.98	1/4	3/4	11/16				
10-14	255.49	+2.78	7/16	1-7/16	1-1/16				
10-15	254.55	-0.94	3/8	1-1/8	15/16				
10-16	258.60	+4.05	11/16	2-3/16	1-5/8				
10-17	258.18	-0.42	9/16	1-7/8	1-5/8				
10-18	257.24	-0.94	3/8	1-7/16	1-1/4	13/16			
10-21	256.19	-1.05	1/4	1-3/16	7/16	7/16			
10-22	257.21	+1.02	7/16	1-1/2	1-5/16	9/16	1/4		
10-23	257.50	+0.29	1/2	1-11/16	1-7/16	1/2	3/16		
10-24	256.11	-1.39	1/4	1-1/4	1-1/4	7/16	3/16		
10-25	–	–	–	–	–	–	–		
10-28	255.94	+1.16	1/4	13/16	15/16	–	–		
10-29	258.01	+2.07	3/8	1-7/16	1-1/4	9/16	3/16		
10-30	259.62	+1.61	7/16	1-13/16	1-11/16	5/8	–		
10-31	259.25	-0.37	3/8	1-7/16	1-7/16	1/2	3/16		
11-1	261.94	+2.69	11/16	2-5/8	2-1/16	3/4	1/4		
11/4	262.34	+0.40	5/8	2-9/16	2-1/16	11/16	3/16		
11/5	26⌀		7/8	3-5/8	2-7/16	7/8	5/16		
11/6	26⌀ ②	0.23	7/8	4	2-1/2	7/8	3/16 ③		
11/7	262.76	-1.05	11/16	3-1/4	2-5/16	3/4	3/16		
11/8	264.26	+1.50	1-3/16	4-3/4	3	1-1/8	5/16		
11-11	269.47	+5.21	4-3/8	9-5/8	6 .	2-7/8	1		
11-12	270.46	+0.99	5-5/8	10-3/4	7-1/8	4	2		
11-13	269.10	-1.36	4-1/8	9	6-3/8	3-5/8	1-3/4		
11-14	271.88	+2.78	6-7/8	11-3/4	8	4-3/4	2-5/16	15/16	5/16
11-15	270.74	-1.41	5-3/4	11-1/4	6-7/8	4	1-13/16	7/8	3/8
11-18	271.31	+0.57			7-3/8	4-1/8	2	13/16	3/8
11-19	271.17	-0.14			7-1/8	4	1-3/4	11/16	1/4
11-20	271.91	+0.74			8-1/8	4-5/8	2-1/16	13/16	1/4
11-21	275.70	+3.79			11-1/8	6-7/8	3-5/8	1-7/16	9/16
11-22	275.42	-0.28			11-1/8	6-1/2	3-1/2	1-3/8	1/2
11-25	273.66	-1.76			9-7/8	5-5/8	2-11/16	1	1/4
11-26	274.85	+1.19			10-5/8	6	2-7/8	1-1/16	3/8
11-27	279.34	+4.39			15-1/4	10	6	2-13/16	1

297

The market continued to move higher through December, and the Index Option table for the close on

Monday December 16, 1985.

American Exchange

MAJOR MARKET INDEX

Strike Price	Calls—Last Dec	Jan	Feb	Puts—Last Dec	Jan	Feb
245	1/16	.....	....	....	....	....
250	....	44	....	....	1/16	....
255	39	39	....	....	....	....
260	36	37¾	....	....	....	3/16
265	31	33	....	....	1/16	7/16
270	26¼	28	....	1/16	5/16	¾
275	21¼	23½	23½	1/16	11/16	1⅝
280	16	18½	20½	⅛	1⅛	2½
285	11	14½	15½	¼	2 1/16	3½
290	6½	10¼	12	3/16	3⅜	5⅛
300	13/16	5	7⅜	5⅜	8	...

Total call volume 75,645 Total call open int. 97,643
Total put volume 42,174 Total put open int. 148,723
The index: High 297.55; Low 291.21; Close 296 ,+4.53

December 16, 1985 (courtesy of the **Wall Street Journal**) gives us the full extent of the profit if held to that date.

The Major Market Index had moved up to ***296*** (arrow), where the ***275*** Call was worth ***21***, and was actually selling at ***21-1/4*** (arrow).

1 Index Option at 21-1/4 is worth $2,125

10 Index Options at 21-1/4 are worth $21,250

100 Index Options at 21-1/4 are worth $212,500

and *233* Index Options at 21-1/4

are worth $495,125

With the November 265/December 275 Call Option Pyramiding, an initial investment of *$937* had become worth *$495,125* in little more than two months.

It is to be noted that whereas *buying* spots at very low prices for Index Options can be pinpointed, where to *sell* is an entirely different concept.

Thus, in Dollar Averaging, when we view the market situation as appropriate, we typically give the Put or Call advice to: "Buy the Option of the near-month (or middle-month in some cases) closest to the *1/2* level, and after making that purchase, place open orders to buy equal dollar amounts at 1/4, 1/8 and 1/16."

This is definitive and automatic. That was how we hit the two very large successes described in previous pages — the $1,062 to $63,000 move with the February 255 Call Options in early-1987, and the $2,000 to $192,400 move with the October 285 Put Options, right before the October 1987 market crash. And there were many suc-

299

cesses of smaller dimensions along the same lines, which utilized this same Dollar Averaging "formula" in previous years.

With *Pyramiding*, this is essentially "catching a wave," just as a surfboarder tries to do! Here, there is a move of some power under way in the stock market, whether to the upside, or the downside, and if we see a promising "wave" at hand, we recommend buying a specific Index Option, and when it has developed a good profit, and we feel the market will continue in the same direction, because of the momentum the move has developed, we counsel, in effect, jumping off one surfboard on to another, in mid-flight!

That was how the November 265/December 275 Call Options worked in 1985.

Where And How To Take Profits

In the case of both Dollar Averaging and Pyramiding, when a substantial profit is at hand, one needs to have a rational approach as to where to take those profits.

A valuable approach is to use a "Trailing Stop Loss Order." This happens to be a very practical and *successful* approach in *common stock speculation*. In that case, you buy a stock when the technical evidence indicates an upside breakout. As soon as the purchase is made, you place a "stop loss" order under the purchase price, to automatically limit your loss to the predetermined figure. If success is achieved, and the stock lifts off to the upside, you want to protect the profit that is developing.

To do this, you place a stop order *below* the higher prices as they develop — say 5% below. If the stock drops back by 5%, your stock is sold, and you retain the balance of the profit that had developed.

If the profit *continues* to mount, with the stock moving still higher, you continuously *raise* the price of the stop order, staying approximately 5% below the last price. If the stock continues to run, your profit continues to mount, and you know that if a reversal takes place and the stock begins to decline, you will be "stopped out" approximately 5% below the high, safeguarding your accumulated profit.

In the case of *Index Options*, the Index Price serves the same purpose as the price of the stock. You choose an appropriate percentage decline for your stop order, using the guidelines of "Technical Analysis," and if the Index falls by that amount you are, once again, "stopped out," safeguarding your profit at a high level.

This approach takes full advantage of a *powerful* move (such as occurred, for example, in November/December 1985), because if the market continues to surge higher, your "trailing stop loss order" *also* continues to move higher, with the Index.

Thus, a very workable approach to "where to take profits"!

The Importance Of Keeping A Daily Option Record

There is no question that any reader keeping a daily record of Index Options, in the way we shall now describe, will find results greatly improved! When you put something down with your own hand, *it registers in your mind*, and you begin to absorb the relationship of Index Option price movement to the movement of the market, and even the movement of one Index Option to another Index Option.

There is nothing complicated about such a table, which is *a series of columns*. Your put the date in the first column, the close for the Index you are following in the second column, the change in the Index for the day in the third column, and then the Index Options which need watching, one column for each.

These, typically, are the near-month (due to expire on the third Friday of that month), and the middle-month, focusing on the *low-price* Index Options which are, by definition, "out of the money," and provide the greatest leverage.

Look at the table we were keeping in 1985, as shown on page 297, to get an idea of how it should be done. When the *November 265* Call Option was moving up, we could be thinking of where to take profits, and when a good selling price coincided with the *December 275* Call Options selling at 3/16, the mind was jogged to consider a Pyramiding approach. Thus the value of such tables.

Dramatic Opportunities Ahead

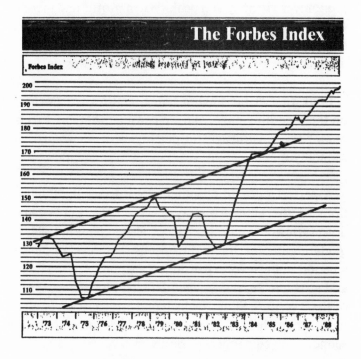

As we are writing these words, in July 1989, we consider that both the economy and the stock market are "doing a high-wire act," and we are certain that both are going to fall off that wire.

By letting a mountain of debt grow during the past few decades, and particularly since 1981, when the "Reagan Era" commenced, we have put ourselves in a position where *any* recession will find economic distress growing very rapidly.

303

The point is that a very large number of debtors can hardly manage their debts as we write, when the economy is virtually at a peak. When profits and income go into decline as a recession takes hold, many of these debtors will have to sell off assets to stay afloat, and a domino type of action will begin to the downside.

Look first at the **Forbes Index** (courtesy of **Forbes**), on the preceding page, and we consider that chart to be one of the most insightful portrayals of the total U.S. economy.

A perfect uptrend Channel encompasses the fluctuations of the U.S. economy 1973 - 1984, but when a downturn would have been to excellent effect in 1984, liquidating the inevitable distortions that develop during a period of business expansion, the stimulus of the huge, and growing, federal budget deficits, plus the workings of the "Welfare State," which had grown to encompass more than half of the population, propelled the economy on to dangerous heights.

Those heights are dangerous (that is where we are now), because in any market economy, recessions are both *unavoidable* and *normal*. They are also *desirable*! But if recessions are postponed because of debt creation (debt creates money with a built-in *multiplier*) then the recession which finally comes is deeper, more threatening. Towards that end, the chart shown (courtesy of **Fortune**), spells out better than anything else could, the deep troubles that are ahead. The chart is the total of

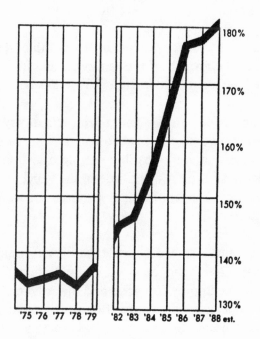

'75 '76 '77 '78 '79   '82 '83 '84 '85 '86 '87 '88 est.

OFF THE CHARTS
**Credit card companies can't turn out
enough plastic. During the 1980s government and private debt broke into new
territory, climbing to nearly $9 trillion.**

Total debt as a percent of GNP

305

public and private debt as *a percent of Gross National Product*, putting into the discard the argument that, yes, debts have grown, but so has the economy.

It has been clear for years that the growth of debt was outpacing the growth of the economy, and in the chart you see how *steep* that fevered growth has been.

We are, indeed, *neck-deep* in debt, and any recession will hold grave dangers of gathering momentum towards a *deep* recession, very possibly verging over into a full-scale depression on a worldwide basis, which will hold *large* political dangers in many parts of the world, for U.S. interests.

Because this is so, we have not the slightest doubt that Chairman Greenspan and the entire Federal Reserve Board, backed up by Congress and the Administration, will be opening the credit floodgates to turn the economy around, once recession has proceeded to a certain point.

This will *cause another inflation spiral*, but it is much easier to handle debt during a period of inflation, than during a *deflation*, which itself holds very great dangers. What we have just described will lead to a sharply *down* market (the onset of recession), followed by a sharply *up* market (Fed action), and cause a long period of very sharp market moves.

A down-then-up stock market is *made-to-order* for

high-leveraged moves among the hundreds of long-term *Warrants* trading today. Meanwhile, sharp market moves are similarly *"made-to-order"* for high-leverage, very low-price *Index Options*.

Further, the more than 900 Convertible Bonds and Convertible Preferred Stocks will constitute very flexible market instruments with which to *conserve* capital, and *enhance* capital, through the ups and downs of what we have described.

Consequently, all the preceding pages in this book will prove highly useful to the reader in minimizing risk and maximizing profit potential, with **Warrants, Options** and **Convertibles!**

CURRENT SUPPLEMENT AVAILABLE

As this book was going to press, important developments were taking place. Long-Term *Warrants* on dozens of the most important Japanese companies, already trading in Europe, will, before too long, trade in the United States as well.

Stock Index *Futures* and Stock Index *Options* on the Japanese stock markets are already trading in Japan and elsewhere, and are preparing to trade in the United States. They will be highly-important speculative mediums, along the lines set forth in this book.

In the **Current Supplement,** the latest approaches to Index Option speculation are described, in light of the most recent stock market action.

In addition, the Current Supplement contains a valuable alphabetical listing by *Industry Group,* of all Warrants, Convertibles and Scores trading today, plus other current information important in today's market, regarding these fields.

The publishers of this book would like to send you this Current Supplement. Just send your name and address to:

Current Supplement, Department 96
R.H.M. Press
172 Forest Avenue
Glen Cove, New York 11542

There is no cost or obligation.